Industrial Renaissance

Industrial Renaissance

Producing a Competitive Future for America

WILLIAM J. ABERNATHY

KIM B. CLARK

ALAN M. KANTROW

OF THE HARVARD BUSINESS SCHOOL

Basic Books, Inc., Publishers   New York

4214

Library of Congress Cataloging in Publication Data

Abernathy, William J.
  Industrial renaissance.

  Includes index.
  1. Technological innovations—United States.
  2. Industrial productivity—United States.
  3. Automobile industry and trade—United States—
Technological innovations. 4. Competition,
International. I. Clark, Kim B. II. Kantrow,
Alan M., 1947–   III. Title.
  HC110.T4A58 1983   338.4'5   82–72391
  ISBN 0–465–03254–0

Copyright © 1983 by Basic Books, Inc.
Printed in the United States of America
Designed by Vincent Torre
10 9 8 7 6 5 4 3 2 1

For Claire, Sue, and Jane,

whose patience is exceeded

only by their understanding

and their understanding only by

their generosity of spirit

Contents

Acknowledgments

DURING the course of the multi-year research effort that has, at last, led to the present volume, we have been remarkably fortunate in the unflagging support we have received from three venerable institutions and the unusually able men who run them: the Harvard Business School and its dean, John McArthur; the school's Division of Research and its director, Raymond Corey; and the *Harvard Business Review* and its editor, Kenneth Andrews. We have also been fortunate in the sound advice and counsel we have received from those friends and colleagues both at Harvard and the Massachusetts Institute of Technology who reviewed, criticized, and thereby vastly improved the present manuscript at one or another stage of its evolution: Richard Rosenbloom, Robert Hayes, Earl Sasser, Robert Stobaugh, George White, John Bishop, Margaret Graham, Alfred Chandler, Thérèse Flaherty, Malcolm Salter, James Utterback, and Martin Anderson. To Hugh Miller and Marlene Phillips at the National Academy of Engineering we express a special word of thanks, for much of the research here presented draws on work done for the Academy's panel on the automobile industry and its recent report, "The Competitive Status of the U.S. Auto Industry."

To those many individuals in business, academia, government, and labor—both here and in Japan—who answered our questions, smoothed the path of our field research, and tested our developing notions against their own experience, we are deeply grateful. They are, quite literally, too numerous to mention, but we single out the following for their efforts above and beyond the call: Richard John of the U.S. Department of Transportation, Donald Ephlin of the United Auto Workers, James Bakken and William Harahan of Ford, Richard Davis of General Motors, George Butts of Chrysler, Koichi Shimokawa of Keio University, and Mikio Matsui and Takahiro Fugimoto of Mitsubishi Research.

Special appreciation goes, as well, to four of the best research assistants any authors were ever privileged to have: John Corcoran, Mark Thomas, Russell Radford, and Jay Henn. Susan McWade, Janet Litster, and Mary Murphy know perfectly well that none of this would have been possible without their tireless attention to the infinite mechanics of a research project and the infinite labors of producing a final text. They have been, of course, invaluable. To them, as to the others here named, our most sincere appreciation and thanks.

Preface

OUR STARTING POINT in the discussion that follows is a single harsh but inescapable fact: the nation's lackluster industrial performance in recent years is, in large part, the result of the failure of many of its traditional manufacturing industries to adjust to a troubling new set of competitive realities. In some quarters it is still little short of heresy to attribute this loss of vitality to the collapse of the advantage American industry has long enjoyed by virtue of its unexcelled manufacturing competence. We believe, however, that the evidence for this attribution is sufficiently powerful—and its implications sufficiently disturbing—that the time has come to question the established "faith" directly.

In doing so we have chosen to base our argument primarily on a detailed examination of the automobile industry. This approach offers a number of benefits and one major problem. The benefits are obvious: by probing intensively into the workings of a single industry, we are able to examine matters microscopically and to trace general concerns to their most concrete manifestations. Unfortunately, the problem is equally obvious: we are left to argue by inference that what holds true for the automobile industry holds true for other industries as well. This, of course, is not the kind of argument that ought be made without adequate qualification, yet defining the precise terms in which the experience of U.S. auto producers applies to the idiosyncratic situations of other industries is not an easy task.

We will face this problem directly by noting, first, that the circumstances in which the auto producers find themselves are characterized by increased competitive pressures from abroad that have, at their root, high levels of manufacturing performance *and* by a great ferment in product as well as process technology. For managers, this new and highly charged situation presents the formidable challenge of regaining excellence in the management of production systems and technology, and—especially—both together. Where the performance of the U.S. auto industry has grown sluggish with past successes, re-achieving this kind of excellence is more difficult still, because its managers do not start from fresh ground but must first rid themselves of outdated assumptions, practices, and prejudices.

The combination of technology- and production-based competition affecting the auto industry does not apply in equal and balanced measure to every other industry or even to every other manufacturing industry. Even where the "fit" is good, there is no necessary sharing of all the relevant aspects of automobile production: the technological complexity of the product, for example, or the reliance on assembly and fabrication work, or the requirement of operating at high levels of volume. Nonetheless, it is fair to say that many industries do share these aspects and that, the more they do, the more our specific findings about the automobile industry will have relevance for them. The point we are trying to make is fairly simple: our analysis will have varying levels of applicability to other industries.

Our purpose, after all, is not to dwell on automotive data for their own sake but to use the experience of a single industry to reflect heightened understanding on a number of others. We do this with a certain amount of confidence because the main focus of our attention is less the auto industry itself than the more general processes of management and competitive adjustment of which its experience is an example. In minute detail, of course, the Ford Motor Company's approach to quality control at a single engine plant in the Midwest does not necessarily match that of an appliance manufacturer in the South. But as a case in point, it does have a broad representative value of what sound production management entails in today's environment. Put simply, the real center of gravity in what we have to say is the effort to construct a general way of thinking about the competitive significance of technological change as it affects the evolution of production systems. The details may be industry specific, but the conceptual framework is not.

PART I

Toward a Production- and Technology-Based Competition

Chapter 1

The New Industrial Competition

IT IS just barely possible that, in some remote corner of the United States, a latter-day Rip van Winkle awoke this morning with shining images of American industry as it existed in the 1950s still proudly fixed in his head. But it is not likely. Who, after all, could have slept undisturbed through the recent chorus of lament about the economy? Who could have remained unaware that much of U.S. industry—especially in the mature manufacturing sector—had fallen on hard times? Who could have missed the fact that the very basis of industrial competition had changed—and changed radically?

And who did not have a sure-fire remedy? Born-again supply siders argued for a massive formation of capital and a trickle-down (or, as John Kenneth Galbraith would have it, a "horse-and-sparrow") approach to economics; "new class" advocates of industrial policy, for the better allocation of existing capital; industrial economists, for enhanced productivity; trust-busting regulators, for an end to comfortable oligopoly; organized labor, for job security; subdued if unrepentant Keynesians, for more artful demand management; boisterous Lafferites, for a massive tax cut; congressional experts, for carefully targeted tax breaks on depreciation and investment; fee-hungry middlemen, for lucrative leaseback provisions; Friedmanites, for tight money; Naderites, for an anticorporate economic democracy; and bedlamites, for some of each.

This loudly divided counsel on the best strategy for managing economic change reflects a certain troubling inadequacy in both perception and understanding. Of course, we do not mean that a good case cannot be made for some of these patent remedies. We mean, rather, that the sheer cacophony of prescription is itself evidence of a broad-based failure of interpretation, an inability or unwillingness to see that our current economic malaise defies the, by now, standard categories of analysis and discussion.

To date, two main distinctions have provided the structure for that discussion.[1] The first is the division between analysis and prescription of a "macro" sort (that is, having to do with such overarching questions of economic management as fiscal and monetary policy and tax incentives) and those of a "micro" sort (that is, having to do with issues relating to management of particular companies). The second is the division between analysis and prescription based on "software" (people management, organizational systems, and corporate strategies) and those based on "hardware" (equipment, plants, buildings, and machinery).

Considered together, these divisions form the simple matrix shown in table 1.1. Although the distinctions among quadrants are rough, they are nonetheless useful. In practice, however, they are often neglected, which has left the unfortunate impression in some minds that industrial difficulties are composed equally—and indistinguishably—of problems in all the quadrants. This impression has been mischievous, for neither problems nor remedies are distributed evenly about the matrix.

The belief that they are so distributed is itself the result of a common, though often misleading, tendency to halve the difference in any dispute. There is a certain appealing neatness in having things turn out this way, but the appeal is aesthetic only, the attraction of orderly arrangements. In the real world of messy and often lopsided fact, symmetry is a welcome but infrequent guest. As Mark Twain's irrepressibly opinionated character Pudd'nhead Wilson observes, "Behold the fool saith, 'Put not all thine eggs in the one basket'—which

TABLE 1.1

Key Elements of Manufacturing Competitiveness

	Macro	**Micro**
Hardware	I. Government Fiscal and Monetary Policies Taxation Capital markets Savings	II. Production Capability Plant Equipment
Software	III. Socioeconomic Environment Work ethic Regulation Education	IV. Corporate Management Organization Administration Production systems

4

is but a manner of saying, 'Scatter your money and attention'; but the wise man saith, 'Put all your eggs in the one basket and—WATCH THAT BAS-KET.' "

In our judgment, the basket most in need of watching today is the cluster of management practices in quadrant IV (table 1.1). Issues in the other quadrants are important, to be sure, but we believe that "micro software"—what management does—is essential to the renaissance of a beleaguered American industry. This belief may occasion surprise in some quarters, for it assumes that American manufacturers have gotten into trouble not because of general economic conditions or unfair trade practices but because they lost the determination to manufacture well. In other quarters—among, say, true believers in the eternal supremacy of American production—the merest whisper of such a belief is rank heresy.

During the 1930s, for example, when the ability of America's economic system to provide an acceptable standard of living fell under serious question, the essential weakness of that system—the rottenness at its core—was often linked in the popular mind either to the figure of a callous, cigar-chomping industrialist, who played like an indifferent god with the livelihood of hard-working men, or to the figure of a spoiled, pampered, and obnoxiously wealthy consumer, who would dine nightly at the Plaza while others went hungry.

F. Scott Fitzgerald, that consummate novelist of twentieth-century manners, limns an unforgettable portrait of one of these parasites of consumption at the top of the economic heap:

[She] bought from a great list that ran two pages, and bought the things in the windows besides. Everything she liked that she couldn't possibly use herself, she bought as a present for a friend. She bought colored beads, folding beach cushions, artificial flowers, honey, a guest bed, bags, scarfs, love birds, miniatures for a doll's house and three yards of some new cloth the color of prawns. She bought a dozen bathing suits, a rubber alligator, a travelling chess set of gold and ivory, big linen handkerchiefs . . . , two chamois leather jackets of kingfisher blue and burning bush from Hermès—bought all these things not a bit like a high-class courtesan buying underwear and jewels, which were after all professional equipment and insurance—but with an entirely different point of view. [She] was the product of much ingenuity and toil. . . . She illustrated very simple principles . . ..[2]

To Fitzgerald, as to many of his contemporaries, these principles formed the catechism of moral bankruptcy—not of the economic system as a whole, but merely of some individuals within it. The voices that sought to indict all that American capitalism had built may have been loud, but they were loud out of proportion to their numbers. That the muscle and sinew of industry could be misused, that its bumper crops of hard products and harder cash could be distributed unfairly, that the set of values underpinning its work could be profoundly misguided—these were the driving suspicions and, at times, the convictions of a hard-pressed public. But even with better people in the industrial saddle, with a fairer scheme to distribute what they made, and with a more compassionate view of what their responsibilities were, the system could still not be made to work successfully—this was the lament of a small and isolated minority. Put at the service of better men and better ideals, American industry promised to be an indefatigable engine of progress.

A generation later, after a great war had been fought and won by the mobilization of both high principle and industrial might, that promise seemed fulfilled. Who could remain in doubt? America had clearly shown itself to be what its bounteous natural resources, geographical advantages, and national character had long foretold: an "affluent society" and a "people of plenty." If nineteenth-century Americans had thought the continent theirs by right of manifest destiny, their post–World War II descendants thought themselves entitled to ever-increasing economic abundance. With the once-troublesome "problem of production" largely solved, industry could turn its primary attention to the division of the spoils.

This happy industrial landscape is, as we have all too good reason to know, not at all what our latter-day Rip van Winkle would see about him in the 1980s. And if, in confusion, he were to listen to the voices busily trying to explain to him what had gone wrong, he would discover that lackluster industrial performance was related to everything, was caused by everything, influenced everything, and could be cured by everything—except nothing worked. Rip would now be more confused than ever. If inescapable forces had driven American industry on the rocks, how was it possible that some industries and some companies had not only escaped disaster but sailed serenely on? Genuine ocean swells show no favoritism. Further, how was it possible that much the same forces operating on other national economies had not produced the same degree of wreckage? Both Japan and Germany, for example, imported a far higher percentage of their energy needs than did the United States; transfer payments in many European societies outdistanced those here. A falling tide, as President Kennedy did not have to observe during the salad days of the 1960s, lowers all the ships. When some continue to ride high in the water while others list dangerously on the shoals and still others lie grounded on the beach, then it is time to look elsewhere for an explanation of the nation's industrial shipwreck.

Only recently have some observers begun to think that the heart of the problem might lie not in one or another momentary disruption in the steady march of economic progress but in a profound transformation in the nature of industrial competition itself. Perhaps the threat of competitive defeat had so drawn

6

attention to a hairsplitting interpretation of the established rules that participants and onlookers both were slow to discover that the rules themselves had changed.

Indeed, a change of this sort is precisely what we think has occurred, and the magnitude of its implications is only now beginning to come into focus. Most obviously, the safe haven of the American domestic market no longer provides shelter against the rigors of increasingly global competition. Not only have foreign producers, most notably the Japanese, made substantial inroads into U.S. markets; the whole logic of achieving high levels of performance has shifted to accommodate the new realities of worldwide competition.

At the same time, moreover, technical advances have both changed the accepted rules of play and changed the way the rules are changed. Our recently awakened Rip would, no doubt, be amazed that the major competition for established commercial banks and white-shoe investment banks came not from others of their ilk but from aggressive brokerage houses like Merrill-Lynch, retail merchants like Sears, purveyors of money market funds like Fidelity, and providers of consumer credit like American Express. He would also find it puzzling that the evolution of key industrial products—for example, the 64-K semiconductor chip—could occur so rapidly that only the first few players on the scene could justify their investment. And he would marvel that the underlying technology of some of the bluest of blue chip corporate names (such as Kodak's in chemical-based imaging) might suddenly threaten to become obsolete.

Perhaps more than anything else, Rip would be struck by the renewed competitive importance of differential excellence in manufacturing. Over the years American managers had grown so used to thinking of their major task as the marketing, under strict and analytic financial controls, of what their factories effortlessly brought forth, that they had lost touch with the actual work of production. More to the point, they had lost touch with the notion that skill in production, not just in marketing or finance, could offer a real competitive advantage. Bemused and beguiled with the latest fashions in discounted cash flow analysis and the like, they had often overlooked the strategic importance of manufacturing and had, in effect, managed their way to economic decline.[3]

Early in F. Scott Fitzgerald's *The Great Gatsby,* Nick Carraway has the following conversation with Jordon Baker, a lovely but ethically suspect young woman:

"You're a rotten driver," I protested. "Either you ought to be more careful, or you oughtn't to drive at all."
"I am careful."
"No, you're not."

7

"Well, other people are," she said lightly.
"What's that got to do with it?"
"They'll keep out of my way," she insisted. "It takes two to make an accident."
"Suppose you met somebody just as careless as yourself."
"I hope I never will," she answered.[4]

So, too, with strategically suspect American managers. As long as the general postwar pattern of competition remained in force, their inattention to the work of production had relatively little effect. When, however, that pattern changed, they could only reap the bitter harvest of their idle neglect. One can, of course, get away for a while with driving a car badly or on the wrong side of the road—until, that is, traffic appears from the opposite direction. Then past carelessness rather suddenly becomes life-threatening.

And threatening indeed are the new terms of industrial competition: the appearance of aggressive, globally-oriented opponents, the speeding up of the competitive effects of technological change, and the heightened importance of excellence in manufacturing. But there is something else, too. In the past when the nation's economy faltered or particular industries fell upon hard times—and let us not forget how frequent such occurrences were—the pain of industrial dislocation hurt every bit as much as it hurts today. But, unlike today, the fact that such dislocations could occur occasioned no surprise. What now proves so difficult to accept is not the harsh reality of economic suffering but the overthrow of a set of assumptions that, although fairly recent in origin, has nonetheless come to seem an inalienable part of the American way of life.

We have come to take for granted, to accept as the norm of our experience, the nation's industrial growth during the first two decades after World War II. That the economy was and would ever be an unfailing engine of bounty, that standards of living would constantly increase, that the kingpins of industry—the GM's and U.S. Steel's—were so strong that they could endure with impunity any amount of taxation or regulation, that the task of federal policymakers was not, as in other societies, the allocation of scarcity but the equitable sharing of abundance—these were the principles of our historically short-sighted faith. We looked into the manufacturing accomplishments of a few remarkable years and thought we saw reflected there the whole course of our future development.

It was as if American society had accidently stumbled across a remarkably fertile goose, one that never seemed to tire of laying golden eggs. True, no one really knew why or how the goose did what it did, but who was to complain? The gold was there for all to enjoy, and there would always be more tomorrow. In fact, the only thing society had to worry about was the extent of the demand for its precious eggs—not whether the demand would be too great, but whether it would be too little. Fortunately enough, therefore, the goose found its way to a laying house so well equipped with all the modern instruments of mass persuasion that consumer demand could be generated at need to absorb whatever the blessed bird produced. That it would produce was never in question; in recent memory it always had. That it would continue to do so seemed inevitable.

Today, of course, this happy illusion lies shattered. Like a rich child away at school whose allowance—received weekly in the mail—has suddenly and mysteriously been cut off, all those who believed in the unquestioned primacy of American manufacturing now find themselves abandoned by events. The harsh truth is that the industrial landscape in America is already littered with the remains of once-successful companies that could not adapt their strategic vision to altered conditions of competition.

If, today, automobile producers or steel producers or producers in other industries where the new terms of competition apply prove unequal to the reality that confronts them, their teeming plants will become the ghost towns of late twentieth-century America. We speak not only of what has been called smokestack America but of all production-based companies facing the kind of challenge we have described. Only those firms able to see that new mode of competition for what it is and to devise appropriate strategies for participating in it will survive. Macroeconomic forces notwithstanding, managers must recognize that they have entered a period of competition that requires of them a mastery of technology-driven strategy, of efficient and high-quality production, and of competent workforce management. They cannot simply copy what others do but must find their own way. No solutions are certain, no strategies assured of success. But the nature of the challenge is clear.

Henry Ford, as Alfred P. Sloan recalled him, was a man who had "many brilliant insights in his earlier years, but never seemed to understand how completely the market had changed from the one in which he had made his name and to which he was accustomed. The old master failed to master change."[5] That is still the crucial challenge—and opportunity.

II

We believe that the globalization of industry, the acceleration of the technical changes that drive industry maturity, and—especially—the enhanced strategic importance of manufacturing should set the agenda for management action as well as for informed public discussion.[6] History does not treat kindly societies that diagnose their structural weaknesses only after those weaknesses have become irreversible. As Dean Henry Rosovsky of Harvard has observed,

> Most economic historians agree that Britain's climacteric occurred about one hundred years ago, but this fact did not really become a matter of public concern until after World War I. . . . In my opinion, the principal factors were internal and human, and therefore avoidable: British entrepreneurship had become flabby; growth industries and new technology were not pursued with sufficient vigor; technical education and science were lagging; the government-business relationship was not one of mutual support. When we look at our own country today in the perspective of history, the danger signals seem obvious.[7]

Rosovsky makes an excellent point: as with Britain in the past, the mounting evidence of slippage in America's industrial base can be all too easily transformed into the litany of causes cited by future historians for the remorseless decline in our national fortunes. For the historical analogy to hold, all that is necessary on our part is a comparable lack of timely attention to the danger signals. Or so Rosovsky implies. We agree with him but would add another observation to his: the problem for America is not so much to heed the warning signs now being flashed by a few widely agreed-on measures of industrial performance; rather, it is to keep the public consensus on diagnosis and remedy from being immediately captured by those with the loudest voices or the most superficially plausible analyses.

The present difficulties of American industry are not in fact the result of an unstoppable Japan Inc., or the lack of an adequate industrial policy to usher sunset industries into the wings at as low a social cost as possible, or the depredations of "paper entrepreneurs," those parasitic experts who—according to Robert Reich's delicious summary—lay waste their considerable powers in

> establishing joint ventures, consortiums, holding companies, mutual funds; finding companies to acquire, "white knights" to be acquired by, commodity futures to invest in, tax shelters to hide in; engaging in proxy fights, tender splits, spinoffs, divestitures; buying and selling notes, bonds, convertible debentures, sinking-fund debentures; obtaining government subsidies, loan guarantees, tax breaks, contracts, licenses, quotas, price supports, bailouts; going private, going public, going bankrupt.[8]

Whatever such factors actually do contribute to the outward form of industrial suffering, it is no more accurate to attribute to them the cause of that suffering than it is to impute the cause of some rare tropical disease to the fever it brings. Medicine has long known the difference between symptom and cause, and it is high time that discussions of industrial health learned it as well. The nagging discomforts that industry suffers *with* are legion; what it suffers *from,* however, are wrenching structural transformations in the competitive dynamics of its traditional systems of production. And it suffers, as well, from the painful slowness with which management, both public and private, has adjusted to the reality of those transformations.

Although the precise course of events in any one threatened industry does not exactly duplicate that in another, the whole litany of crisis has a disturbingly familiar pattern to it. In color televisions, for instance, newly aggressive foreign competitors emphasized high productivity, reliability, quality, and competent (but not, with the exception of SONY, innovative) design. Many long-established American producers—Warwick, Motorola, and Admiral among them—could not withstand the foreign thrust and were either taken over or went out of business. The manufacturing excellence on which that thrust rested was not achievable only on foreign soil—witness the success, under Sanyo management, of the old Warwick plant with many of the same employees and U.S. middle managers as before.[9]

Much the same inability to respond to outside competition marks the textile machinery business, which before the 1960s was dominated by a few U.S. producers like Draper. When they began to lose their edge in product performance to European and Japanese manufacturers and to fall behind in the application of the newest technical advances, they were not able to regain lost ground. Having been, for the most part, acquired by conglomerates (Draper was taken over by Rockwell International), which treated them as cash cows, the American producers could not make the necessary investment to shore up their former technical or market leadership—and so lost both.

Again, in machine tools, that bellwether component of all industrialized economies, the Germans and later the Japanese made their entrance into the U.S. market with a strategy built around a very reliable, high-quality product. Recently, when a U.S. automobile producer ordered machine tools from an established U.S. manufacturer and from Toyota, both sets arrived at the same time. Toyota, however, sent two engineers who had the equipment running and fully debugged in two weeks, while the competitor's team of eight engineers spent several months getting its equipment operational.

High quality, reliable performance, relatively low cost based on real manufacturing efficiencies—these have been, time and again, at the heart of the competitive strategy that has enabled foreign producers to outflank, outfox, and outperform their American counterparts. Some years back Hokuetsu, a Japanese maker of air compressors, decided to enter its own domestic market, which up until then had been dominated by American producers. Within five years Hokuetsu reduced Ingersoll-Rand's share of the Japanese market from 50 percent to zero by introducing a dependable, good-quality air compressor at half the cost of Ingersoll-Rand's. The incident is dramatic but not unique. In fact, it represents in form if not in degree what has become or may become

11

common in that growing spectrum of industries where the new terms of competition apply: jet engines, commercial aircraft, small forklift trucks, automobile tires, radios, motorcycles, electric motors, lawnmowers, cameras, office copiers, watches, household appliances, electrical switching equipment, hand calculators, and, of course, steel and automobiles and a host of others.

To make matters worse, American competitors in each of these industries are not experiencing a temporary loss of their share in once-and-for-all established markets. Their weakened condition has pushed them toward the sidelines as the industries in which they compete undergo profound technological and structural upheavals. They do not, as in the past, have the luxury of drawing a recuperative breath, slowly plotting to recapture lost ground, and gradually setting to work to right a balance that has turned against them.

The industrial battlefield on which they find themselves is not like that of the first World War, in which evenly matched antagonists struggled back and forth over relatively stable chunks of territory in an agonizingly slow war of attrition. Battle, during the 1980s and beyond, will be on rapidly changing topography, where the identity of the combatants, the nature and focus of the contest, and even the most basic rules of combat can change from minute to minute. Under the new industrial competition, there are no frozen niches in frozen markets for which established producers compete like so many successive dictators in a banana republic. Markets and industries are themselves in flux, and to the winners belong not so much the old-fashioned spoils of victory as the right to define the terms of competition in the future.

III

Nowhere on America's beleaguered industrial front are the harsh implications of this new mode of competition more sharply in evidence than in the parlous fortunes of the domestic automobile producers. So bitter and unexpected have their reverses been that these once proud barons of industry are no longer impregnable in their Detroit fortresses. Lackluster manufacturing operations, failure to adopt a technology- and not just a marketing- based strategy, drastic shifts in customer preferences, and anemic final sales have thrown wide the gates to foreign competitors. Their traditional defenses breached, domestic producers have seemed unable to staunch the hemorrhaging of cash flow that, by reducing working capital and liquidity, weakens still further their capacity to resist.

Already the bleak reminders of unfavorable battles pockmark the landscape.

Plants stand idle; huge numbers of both blue- and white-collar employees are out of work; suppliers, strapped beyond endurance, begin to wither and die; whole regions of the country fall into serious decay. This is not rhetorical flourish. No modern society can easily or painlessly absorb the destruction of an industrial base that, until quite recently, kept some 30,000 suppliers healthy by pumping $40 billion a year of purchase orders onto their books; that employed a large fraction of the nation's work force; that accounted for much of the nation's consumption of raw materials like rubber, steel, aluminum, copper, lead, iron, and zinc; and that made products equivalent to roughly 8 percent of the nation's GNP and 25 percent of its total retail sales. In fact, so deeply and pervasively linked is that industrial base to the economic well-being of the nation as a whole that simplistic arguments to let it fade away, as—some argue—all sunset industries must, remind us of nothing so much as a doctor suggesting to a chronically ill patient that he view his heart and lungs as sunset organs, which ought be allowed to fail without suffering the needless interference of strong medicine.

As the repository of immense production capacity and extensive technological sophistication, the automobile industry remains—as it was during World War II—a prime guarantor of national security through its ability to shift to the production of military equipment. As a ready supporter and consumer of advances in CAD/CAM (computer-assisted design and computer-assisted manufacturing) technology, for example, or lasers or new materials like ceramics or industrial robots, it continues to function as a prime stimulant to innovation. And as the maker of a product whose customers often demand high performance, it has itself acted as a generous sponsor to technological change.

The automobile industry, then, offers us a particularly rich and fertile occasion for exploring in more general terms the recent difficulties and future prospects of those manufacturing industries faced with the new industrial competition. Much as anthropologists do not study a village but study *in* a village, our purpose in the account that follows is to study *in* the automobile industry. To be sure, we will have many detailed things to say about the production of automobiles, but our true object will be to develop as fully as we can a conceptual framework for analyzing and understanding what that new mode of competition means, what it will require of managers in the years ahead, and what promise it holds for a revitalization of the nation's economic health.

Accordingly, we need to fashion a cogent way of thinking about the complex relations among technology, production management, markets, and competition as they change both over historical time and through the course of an industry's evolution. We need to understand the conditions under which and the means by which manufacturing industries can find—and are finding—in the new industrial competition an opportunity for renewal, not merely a threat of extinction. And we need to identify the best way to tell whether, in any given case, such an opportunity exists and is being followed. It is to these efforts that we address ourselves in the hope that heightened understanding may help plant the seeds for a renewed commitment to managerial excellence as well as nurture the encouraging developments already underway. If future efforts can only fulfill current promise, the last decades of this century will see a true renaissance of American industry.

Chapter 2

The Logic of
De-Maturity

ALTHOUGH facing up to the realities of this new industrial competition is likely to prove an unpleasant task, the nation's economic health depends upon it. Many otherwise responsible leaders, however, have apparently decided to try the experiment of addressing the problem by denying that it exists. This experiment has, as a rule, taken one of two forms. The first, which we call the "natural consequences of maturity" view of things, has a deceptively cogent analysis to offer. According to its advocates, what has happened of late to the automobile and other manufacturing industries is, quite simply, the natural consequence of life-cycle processes operating internationally on mature industrial sectors.[1] Much as biological organisms grow and decay, the fortunes of American auto producers have followed a perfectly natural course of development and dissolution. In modern Detroit, as on the blasted heath of King Lear centuries ago, men and all their works "must endure/ their going hence, even as their coming hither./ Ripeness is all." So if in Detroit there is wringing of hands or gnashing of teeth, such lamentation is as useless as it is irrelevant. Neither in Lear's age nor our own has anyone discovered an effective remedy for the inexorable cycles of nature.

Apart from the sheer magnitude of the current drama, or so this view of things would have it, nothing all that remarkable is going on. It may be painful to watch the senescence of once-mighty corporate giants, but such is the inescapable common fate. As with the vigorous domestic producers of radios, television sets, textiles, shoes, and a host of other goods a decade or more ago, the automobile industry has entered at last into the mature stage of its life cycle. Its products have become standardized, virtually a commodity distinguishable only in terms of cost, and its production processes have been embodied in equipment that is available for purchase by all comers. With its mode of production stable and well known, the industry can—and should—do little more than watch the location of factories shift abroad to those geographic areas enjoying advantages in the relative costs of production.

As a matter of public policy, government should not bow to the voices calling on it for relief. It should follow the path of least resistance, so to speak, and let evolution work its will. Hence, to those who believe in the natural consequences of maturity, government's only proper role is to facilitate what is politely called the "positive adjustment" of industry to competitive inevitability. Public officials should not, according to one representative statement, "protect or subsidize industries that are threatened by imports or are otherwise noncompetitive internationally, but should take concrete steps to encourage the transfer of resources from less into more competitive industries."[2] The question of who is sufficiently infallible to be entrusted with the nasty job of picking winners and losers is, not surprisingly, left conveniently unanswered. Neglected as well is the self-fulfilling nature of such choices. To define an industry as a loser is to guarantee that the resources needed to keep it vital will be directed elsewhere.

We overstate, of course. Not all of those who recommend a strategy of positive adjustment intend for there to be any official determination of winning or losing industries. To the contrary, the concern of many is with the actions government might take to ease the wrenching dislocations in labor force and capital markets that will inevitably occur as external competitive forces decide the fate of various industrial sectors.[3] With this more sophisticated approach to industrial policy, we have a good deal of sympathy, but we continue to have grave reservations about the "natural consequences" assumptions on which, to some extent, it rests.

These assumptions are, if anything, closer to the surface and thus more available to critical inspection in a second school of thought, which we call "transient economic misfortune." This, as its name suggests, is a considerably more optimistic reading of the industrial future than that provided by the "natural consequences" school.[4] Its advocates maintain that the present difficulties with automobiles and other hard-pressed industrial groups are temporary, the result of sudden and unpredictable shifts in long-established competitive dynamics. For the auto producers, the heart of the problem is not the cost or quality of their product but inappropriate capacity. Events moved so quickly during the 1970s that they got stuck with too many facilities for building big cars.

The Logic of De-Maturity

To the "transient economic misfortune" school of thought, the only appropriate course of action is to wait for events to right themselves or, perhaps, to give them a little push. Indeed, the forces needed to set the competitive balance back on an even keel are even now locked into place, their happy result merely a matter of time and of bringing the right kind of capacity on line. Nothing has gone wrong except a perfectly understandable misjudgment about capacity, since corrected. The best thing to do is pick a comfortable armchair, dust off that dog-eared novel, put a stack of old favorites on the stereo, and wait confidently for the whole unfortunate incident to pass.

What troubles us most about both these interpretive schemes is that they assume a degree of stability in the technology of manufacturing industries that simply does not exist any longer, if it ever did. Adherents of the maturity thesis take for granted an irreversible tendency of products to become standardized—that is, technologically stable—over time. Adherents of the misfortune thesis, assuming that all outstanding technological problems have been solved, see the automobile industry as needing only to bring the requisite capacity on line to recapture its former competitive standing. Both groups of adherents wind up in error because both argue in too limited a fashion from a set of incomplete assumptions about the relation between industry maturity, on the one hand, and technology, markets, and competition, on the other.

What, then, are these assumptions, and where did they come from? In the first instance, they grew out of work in the fields of marketing and international business.[5] Struck by the intuitive appeal of the biological analogy and by the near-universal tendency of technological innovations to follow an S-shaped curve of diffusion, early researchers sought to define in life-cycle terms the typical biography of manufactured products. Through what definable stages of development did such products pass? What were the usual patterns of cash flow associated with each of these stages? The usual patterns of market penetration? Of plant location? Of product evolution itself?

More recently, William Abernathy, James Utterback, and others have labored to extend the range of consideration to include production processes as well. According to this second generation of research and interpretation, the relevant unit for study is the productive unit or segment. "The essential idea," runs a classic formulation, "is that a . . . productive segment tends to evolve and change over time in a consistent and identifiable manner. That is, as a given productive segment develops over time, it follows a predictable profile that will be common among different industries."[6] And what kind of thing is this segment or unit? Nothing more or less than a given product line and its associated production processes.

As products evolve from low-volume, unstandardized, one-of-a-kind items, their associated production systems evolve from open-ended and unstructured processes toward rigid and elaborately structured processes. In other words, a process/product configuration or productive unit that is initially fluid (relatively inefficient, flexible, and open to radical change) gradually tends over time to become stable (relatively efficient, inflexible, and open only to incremental change).[7] Because different product lines and, more generally, different industries belong at various points along this joint continuum, it is the essence of good management to make certain that the placement in each individual case is optimized. Where deviations from expected placement exist, the manager's responsibility is, therefore, either to correct them to the extent possible or to be certain that they are part of a conscious, well thought through strategy.

No company or industry could long survive the attempt to produce small, highly customized batches of specialty items by employing the kind of dedicated equipment appropriate to the high-volume manufacture of typewriters. By the same token, no large-scale typewriter manufacturer could hope to survive with a job-shop mode of production. These are extreme examples, to be sure, but they make a point: to be competitively successful, manufacturing operations must nicely balance the stages of product and process evolution. Producers of exquisite, one-of-a-kind pieces of jewelry are not likely to lose sleep at night over the need to amass enough capital to purchase equipment for mass production.

Do not forget, however, that there are forces at work in manufacturing industries that tend to drive productive units toward high-volume operations. Head and shoulders above the rest are the benefits to be gained from economies of scale. In the automobile industry, for example, an endless quest for these economies has dictated a search for both ever-greater product standardization and streamlined production. So finely tuned has management's effort been to wring out the last increment of marginal cost reduction that anything threatening to upset the basic technology of process or product has been perceived as a distinct threat to competitive success.[8] Having in the most deliberate manner possible committed themselves to standardization, managers usually believed they had no alternative to sticking with it to the bitter end. As events have shown, the end has been bitter indeed.

Implicit in this belief are substantial assumptions about the nature of the forces at work in the evolution of productive units. In the first instance, these assumptions have to do with the wondrous dynamics of experience curves, which are derived from an elaborate series of observations about the behavior of costs as production volume increases. They hold that, with every doubling of cumulative volume, the cost of each individual unit will fall by something on the order of 25 percent.[9] If true, this fact has important implications for manufacturing strategy. One recent commentator summarizes them this way:

If cost per unit decreases predictably with the number of units produced . . . then the manufacturer with the most units should have the lowest marginal costs. To make more widgets than anyone else, though, one presumably has to sell more widgets, that is, have the largest share of the widget market. The market share leader can underprice competitors by virtue of its lower costs—the result of greater cumulative experience—thereby hastening its drive down the curve. Eventually, market shares will stabilize, nobody new will want to enter the business because of Numero Uno's cost advantage, and the big guy can reap his reward. The overarching lesson seemed clear: go for share.[10]

For thousands of managers, the parable of the good widgetmaker could not have been more explicit. If anything threatens volume, banish it to outer darkness. If doubt arises, banish that too. Remove from your mind all questions about the proper way to produce widgets, ye of little manufacturing faith. Repent and go for volume.

Doubt, however, has not been stilled. The merits of experience curves have for some time now been a subject of heated discussion.[11] Do the curves really give an accurate picture of how costs always behave or of how they behave without vigorous management action? Does their animating logic apply equally well to all sets of competitive circumstances and to all industries? Does it apply equally well to all firms within an industry? What if their implications for a company's strategy require a host of resources—financial, organizational, physical—that either do not exist or cannot conveniently be spared? Can the benefits of experience be acquired through purchase of equipment or technology?

In the face of such nagging problems, to maintain confidence in the general applicability of the curves requires the blanket rejection of doubt. The world according to experience curves is, willy-nilly, on a pilgrimage toward efficient production and industry maturity, and this pilgrimage demands of the faithful a certain attitude toward both process and product technology. With this evolutionary view of technology we are, for good reason, sympathetic; with its dogmatic acceptance as an inflexible and unchangeable model of the way things are and must always be, we have our doubts.

As so often happens with attractive schemes of explanation, what was originally intended as description assumes the status of prescription. It makes quite good sense, we believe, to think about the technology of manufacturing industries as undergoing a process of evolution. It makes no sense, however, to treat that evolutionary process as entirely self-contained or irreversible. Technology does not develop in a vacuum or in isolation from the forces that drive competition within industries. It does not appear from offstage on a cue audible only to itself, like some literal deus ex machina of the modern age. It is not a closed system, obeying no laws but its own.

In the early or "fluid" stage of process/product development, performance criteria for new products are not usually well defined. No one knows for a certainty what the market will want or what the product can or should do. Competitors respond to this lack of agreement by trying out a number of different process/product configurations or designs. Should this new kind of thing called a widget be larger than a breadbox, or would potential users prefer something a bit smaller? Should it be constructed to operate for three months without adjustment, or would it offer no meaningful improvement over pre-widget equipment unless it could run unadjusted for at least six? Should it be built to sell for a hundred dollars, or would a market never materialize unless it sold for under thirty? Could it, for that matter, be built for under thirty? If so, should it be manufactured on the same type of machinery long used in the production of gewgaws, or must there be a new approach to production entirely? Because there are no immediate answers to such questions as these, differences among early widgets will often reflect fundamental differences in technology.

In so experimental a climate, the process of widgetmaking is likely to be flexible, relatively labor-intensive, and somewhat erratic in work flow. With essential questions still unanswered, no manufacturer wants to lock itself into one fixed and unalterable way of doing things or to buy the expensive machinery suited to such a hard-and-fast commitment. As the productive unit evolves and the range of technological possibilities begins to narrow, the diversity among early widgets lessens. This allows a more precise, less flexible, and relatively capital-intensive choice among production alternatives.

Change in product technology, then, is what drives the evolution of widgetmaking. Innovations in product technology that are, in the early stages of development, often radical tend to give way over time to innovations that are technically modest. Further, as standardization of widgetmaking increases, not only the magnitude but also the locus of innovation undergoes a shift. The typical pattern is for early radical changes in product to be replaced by later incremental changes in process—in the progressively intense quest for efficiencies in production that do not threaten to make obsolete ever-higher investments in a given product design or its associated capital equipment. Indeed, innovations at the mature stage of productive-unit evolution are often virtually invisible to anyone save the engineers actually working on the projects.

What are the limitations of this view of things? As we have already suggested, there is a strong presumption that the evolution of a productive unit moves along in only one direction—that widgetmaking inevitably tends to become a mature industry, with all the consequences such maturity holds for industry structure and modes of competition. With manufacturing operations as with anything resembling a biological organism, the process of aging is irreversible.

An industry, once it has reached the mature state of organization, simply cannot recapture the competitive characteristics of its youth. There may be more or less successful ways of confronting the fact of maturity, but there is no way to undo it. Or so runs the conventional assumption. We would argue, however, that here is where the biological analogy finally breaks down, for manufacturing industries can indeed arrest—and in some circumstances even reverse—the maturation process. We would argue for the possibility of industrial "de-maturity."

To be fair, some evolutionary theories do admit the possibility of reversals, but their theoretical defense has been left underdeveloped.[12] The reasons for this neglect are not far to seek: little attention is generally paid to the actual way in which technology evolves in a competitive environment or to the forces that drive that evolution. Observations of the changing nature of technology are usually restricted to an identification of the shift from radical to incremental innovation. So foreshortened a perspective simply does not do justice to the complex interactions of a productive unit with its market and with its underlying technology. To focus on the nature of innovation alone is to miss the mechanics by which the technology of a productive unit becomes competitively significant. And to understand these mechanics is to grasp the possibility of de-maturity.

II

Think for a moment, then, about the way in which the technology of a product actually evolves. The homely but versatile widget is not, on close inspection, a single undifferentiated bundle of technology. It is the consequence of a whole series of technological choices, each of which was made in furtherance of some "design concept"—that is, some particular approach, in technological terms, to the product's basic functional requirements (or "parameters") and, in relation to market demands, to its relevant characteristics (or "attributes").[13] Is the widget to run on electricity or a different source of energy? Is it to be portable or not? Is it to be made from steel or aluminum or plastic? Questions like these define the parameters and attributes of the widget; how they are answered, its design concepts.

No matter how humble, every product is, in an important sense, the sum of a host of responses to such questions. The choice embodied in each response is an attempt to implement what we have called a design concept, and the selection of design concepts for a product is an expression of a company's decision about how to compete. As technology changes and as market preferences shift, the relative importance of the different parameters and attributes shifts as well. Size may have once been a critical matter; now it may be reliability or cost or whatever. Accommodating these adjustments will, of course, place a burden of variable weight on a company's established competence in production. The more the necessary adjustments require change in design concepts, the greater the challenge to manufacturing systems as well as to competitive strategy.

This is not to say that the threat of such change is everywhere the same. Among the design concepts of the widget, for example, there is no equality of importance. There is, instead, what an early minister at Hartford, Connecticut, said of the governance of his congregation: "a speaking aristocracy in the face of a silent democracy." Most commonly, a single "core concept" plays the role of product aristocrat for each set of functional requirements. The choices it represents dominate all others, in that the technical solutions there embodied create a set of givens with which the other solutions must deal. The core concept is particularly trenchant in its effect on all functionally-related design choices; any change in it necessitates change in them or, at least, in most of them. Said another way, it establishes the agenda for a product's technical development along one major functional axis and assumes a distinctive priority in the product's overall evolution.

In the development of the automobile engine, for example, the key functional problem was the selection of the appropriate fuel and, along with it, the operative principle of energy transformation (gasoline versus steam versus electricity). When the core concept became established as internal combustion based on gasoline, the technical agenda was set for a wide range of subsidiary problems and choices compatible with it (cylinder configuration, camshaft and valve placement, and so on). Had the core concept favored electricity, the relevant focus for supporting technology would have been quite different: the physics and chemistry of batteries, say, or the performance characteristics of electric motors.

As core concepts make their appearance in each of a product's major functional domains, the relations among them take on much the same structure as the relations among core and subordinate concepts in the individual domains. A "dominant design" for the product as a whole evolves, within which some functional core concepts are more important, others less. It is, in fact, this analogy between part and whole that links issues of functional design to the evolutionary notions discussed previously. Much as each core concept sets the agenda for its own functional domain, so a product's dominant design establishes an overall hierarchy of technical concern and influence. These hierarchies—at both levels—are important not only because they provide a center of gravity for technical choice, but also because they help provide the means by which a productive unit's technology takes on competitive significance.[14]

Through the establishment of such hierarchies, innovative activity which had earlier been scattered, now crystallizes and moves downward to secondary functional parameters and attributes. In practice, of course, this sequence need not be rigid or linear. Innovations at various points in a functional hierarchy may come in bunches and interact in complex ways. Even so, some will prove more important than others and will attract a disproportionate share of attention. It stands to reason that design concepts at or near the top of a design hierarchy, by virtue of their influence on product function and performance, will have greater competitive visibility than those at the bottom. Hence, market pressures reinforce the internal logic of technical development: only after design concepts at the top of a hierarchy become stabilized does the work of innovation focus on aspects of the product that are not immediately apparent in the marketplace. As already noted, when a product reaches its mature stage of evolution, technological change is often all but invisible.

To speak in this fashion, however, is to tell only part of the story, for the choice among competing design concepts also has substantial implications for production processes. In the early stages of productive-unit evolution, with competition based largely on product performance and with basic changes in technology closely linked to changes in competitive position, flexibility in production is essential. Only when core concepts appear and stabilize the functional hierarchies on which they sit—that is, only with the arrival of standardization in product design—can production processes begin to standardize. For the most part, it is not until a product moves fairly well along toward its mature design stage that the rate of change in process technology begins to outdistance the rate of change in the product itself.[15]

True, as core design concepts "lock in" or stabilize the domain of relevant technical effort, the shifting momentum of innovation allows process development to accelerate. It is also true that a decreasing rate of change in product technology reflects a shift in the basis of competition that rewards more efficient production. Standardization of design implies that, for any given product, the market has agreed that a certain set of design concepts best satisfies many perceived needs. Along with this implication, however, comes another: acquisition of competitive advantage through product innovation becomes ever more difficult. If the market is agreed on an optimal set of design concepts, there is no premium for looking to replace one or more of them with concepts made available through additional research and experimentation. When the market decides that what an automobile is includes a gasoline engine, advanced work on the application of steam propulsion to automobiles has little competitive value.

Standardization of product design changes the basis of competition. Battles in the marketplace no longer are fought over the kind of thing a product is or even the kinds of things it should be able to do. The locus of competition shifts to what the product costs. Once the market decides that it knows what a word processor is—or a video recorder or a PBX exchange or an instant camera or, of course, a widget—the task of manufacturers gradually changes from defining appropriate design concepts to achieving efficiencies and economies in production. This is not to say that product innovation disappears entirely or that it ceases to be of value altogether. The point, rather, is that what product innovation there is tends to be localized toward the bottom of established design hierarchies and, as a consequence, to enjoy little market visibility.

With no premium on change in core concepts and with an ever-larger price tag for such change where it does occur, product innovation comes to play an altered role in competition. Established manufacturers do not entirely give up the search for improved product performance, but they do avoid those directions in which needed innovations require major upheavals in the productive unit. Given this reluctance to upset established operations, innovation in product technology loses much of its earlier appeal. Other things being equal, as companies in an industry become more alike in their production facilities and less willing to disrupt them, the risks of imitation decrease. And if innovations can be easily copied, they then lose their ability to confer competitive advantage.

With this developmental pattern in mind, we can begin to speak of the maturity of a manufacturing industry not in terms of sales growth or the appearance of segmentation in its markets but, rather, in terms of a change in the nature of its technology. A mature industry is one in which an earlier uncertainty has been replaced by a stability in core concepts, a stability that permits process technology to be embodied in capital equipment or in engineering personnel and purchased in the marketplace. By this line of reasoning, the fundamental characteristics of a mature industry are the stability of its technology and the ease with which it can be copied. Thus, to the long familiar rule that competition is the driving force of all industry evolution, we add a new corollary: technological uncertainty, as it occurs on both sides of the market, is the driving force of competition. To those industries—branded consumer goods like soap, for example—where productive unit technology has little competitive effect, our corollary has limited application. But to those industries where technology is closely tied to competitive advantage, our corollary applies quite well.

How to understand the evolutionary processes of this second group of industries? First, on the producer's side, there must be at the outset both a nontrivial set of available product technologies, each with its own distinctive capabilities, and substantial uncertainty about which technologies will best satisfy market needs and preferences.[16] If only a single product technology existed, design concepts would be standardized quite early on; if the capabilities of each technology were identical, choice among them would be irrelevant. In either case, product evolution would be shortcircuited. Then, on the buyer's side, there must be uncertainty both about the mix of services a given set of technologies will deliver and about preferences among them. If potential consumers are not in doubt about which product attributes they will ultimately value more than others (specific dimensions of performance, say, or reliability or appearance), product expectations will be sufficiently clear to produce static behavior in the marketplace. If buyers know from day one precisely what they want in a product as well as which technology can give it to them, competitive evolution is deprived of its motive force. Only when initial uncertainty prevails on both sides of the market will an industry's technology effectively drive its overall development.

When these conditions obtain, a process of iterative searching and learning occurs among producers and buyers alike. For their part, buyers explore the technologies that make possible different product attributes. Not knowing what technical approach or approaches will best meet their as yet uncrystallized preferences, buyers look first to product attributes related to function and performance. As they gain new information, they constantly update their relative valuations of different attributes (is the speed of a widget's operation more important to them, for example, than the length of time it can run without being serviced?) and revise their preferences among technical alternatives (do they really prefer plastic widgets to those made of aluminum?). There is, of course, no reason to suppose that buyers confront the various widget possibilities before them with comparable a priori judgments about what the optimal product technology should be like. Hence, there is no reason to suppose that their assessments of first generation widgets will be identical. Their process of iterative learning will tend to support a wide range of approaches to widgetmaking. With core concepts and design hierarchies still in flux, buyers can—and must—pick their way in and around a substantial amount of technical diversity.

As evidence and experience accumulate, however, that same learning process gradually weeds out unattractive alternatives, thereby reducing uncertainty. How rapidly uncertainty declines is a function of the amount and quality of the information available to buyers. The nature of that information is, in turn, a function of the widget's complexity, durability, and frequency of use. Though uncertainty gives way at different rates with different products (as well as at different stages of the same product's development), give way it does.

The accretion of experience inevitably shrinks the universe of acceptable technological alternatives, for a narrowing of the range of judgments accompanies all learning processes. Beyond a certain point, of course, this emerging market consensus permits the establishment of design hierarchies, based on specific core concepts.

While this iterative learning process among buyers is going on, producers do not stand idly by. To simplify matters a bit, we have spoken of the search and experimentation undertaken by buyers as if both activities were restricted to a constant, finite range of technical options. This is not the case in practice. Producers are engaged in an ongoing search of their own for winning technical combinations, and—like buyers—they learn in an iterative fashion through their failures and successes. Because the early stages of a new product's life are marked by considerable uncertainty about which product attributes the market will value and which design concepts will emerge as core concepts, the needed information can only be generated through market transactions. This notion of "learning by using" maintains that, without making or buying or using products, neither producer nor buyer can acquire critical information about product technology or the ability of that technology to satisfy market preferences.

In short, no advance survey of potential users' likes and dislikes can hope to capture the data generated by introducing a variety of technological approaches into the marketplace. The initial diversity among buyers' judgments will, at the outset, support that variety of approaches; so, too, will the jockeying among producers for accurate information and competitive advantage. How long that diversity lasts will depend, as already noted, on how rapidly learning takes place and on how easily successful design concepts can be imitated. Under such conditions, competitive advantage necessarily accrues to those producers best able to perceive changing market preferences and to develop technology to meet them. Thus, in the early stages of productive-unit evolution, technological diversity and competition based on innovation go hand in hand.

Producers gradually learn to distinguish the relevant product attributes for which they must supply technical solutions acceptable to the market—widget durability, for example, or ease of use or ease of repair. Taken together, these attributes constitute an industry's basis of competition—that is, they define the arena within which different producers stake out their distinctive positions. For some attributes, the positions taken are identical and, as a result, competitively neutral. For most, the positions vary, and this variety fuels the learning process discussed above. Again, for the sake of simplicity, we speak as if the arena itself—the basis of competition—were fixed, the only remaining uncertainty being the choice of position within it. This, of course, is not in fact the case: there is always the possibility that over time new attributes will become important and others will lose their former appeal in the market.

In general, then, competition proceeds along narrowing lines until, in a mature industry, the technological positions taken by the major producers are virtually indistinguishable. The essence of standardization, after all, is the transformation of product attributes that had been competitively significant into ones that are competitively neutral. Attributes that had once been "open" to technical experimentation become over time fixed or "closed," and this process of "closing down" represents—perhaps more clearly than anything else—the evolution of an industry toward maturity.

III

This often-repeated movement from open to closed product attributes suggests a needed revision in the way we typically think about industry maturity and technological change, for maturity, as we have argued, is the process by which competition becomes progressively immune to technology-based change from within the industry. In terms of productive-unit evolution, it is the process by which the drive toward standardization inoculates the unit against competitively significant innovation. That which had been "open" gradually becomes "closed." But this movement toward closure, toward inoculation, and toward immunity does not necessarily run in a single direction. It can be reversed.

How so? We believe that such reversals are not only possible but implicit in the very means by which technology becomes competitively significant in the first place. At the heart of any reversal is a major change in the established relationship between technology and market preferences. For whatever reasons—a sudden shift, say, in the prices of substitute products—a demand may arise among buyers for new dimensions of product performance or for a different set of trade-offs among product attributes. If this demand is sufficiently unlike the one it supersedes, producers may need to seek out new technology, to revise design concepts, to reintroduce innovation as an important element in competition, and to undertake a new round of iterative learning. They may also be confronted by new technologies that make possible entirely new technical approaches to product attributes or previously unattainable levels of product performance. Whether this late-appearing technology is embodied in existing or in substitute products, its effect may be to create a revised set of options for buyers to choose among—and about which they must learn. If so, it will allow producers to stake out once more the grounds for achieving competitive advantage through technology.

No two industries will respond to changes of this sort in identical ways, but it is true nonetheless that a common thread does link all such shifts in preference and technology. The need for reestablishing the "fit" among them upsets usual patterns of purchase and supply and prompts the reemergence of iterative search and learning on both sides of the market. This, in turn, constitutes a reversal of industry development toward maturity—that is, a return to an earlier stage of productive-unit evolution. It is precisely this kind of reversal that we have in mind when we speak of industry de-maturity.

To repeat, a movement toward de-maturity—or away from productive unit standardization—means an increase in the diversity of product technology actually offered in the market as well as an increase in the competitive visibility of that technology. Innovation once more carries a premium, as the focus of innovation shifts back from the refinement of existing concepts toward disruptive change in the concepts themselves. How quickly this shift takes place will vary, but it is not likely to be abrupt. The search for new concepts typically works its way back up through the same design hierarchy established by the evolution toward maturity which preceded it. Changes in core concepts are apt to occur only after changes have already taken place in less fundamental parameters of design. After all, no producer will throw over its vested interests in product design or an existing production process or willingly absorb the expense of bringing a new one on line until it becomes clear that less radical tinkerings with product technology do not have a chance of success in the market.

By its very nature, epochal or disruptive innovation—whatever its degree of technical novelty—makes obsolete existing capital equipment, labor skills, materials, components, management expertise, and organizational capabilities. It destroys the value of present competence in various aspects of production and may alter the relative positions of competitors, attract new entrants into an industry, or even redraw an industry's competitive boundaries. Because epochal innovation works its effects not so much by virtue of technical novelty but by striking at the basic competence of producers, the magnitude of those effects depends on the evolutionary stage of the relevant productive unit. A technical concept that would have offered little disruption in the early phases of a product's development may prove disruptive indeed if it arises after a dominant design has been established and design hierarchies have locked into place. The stabilization of design concepts, in which industry maturity consists, makes productive units increasingly vulnerable to changes in technology, market preference, and relative prices. As does a biological species that has become perfectly adapted to a particular environmental niche, mature industries carry with them the implicit threat of extinction or, at least, catastrophe if environmental conditions should suddenly or radically shift.

In a sense, then, maturity invites de-maturity as a response to nontrivial environmental change. Where the change in external circumstances is moderate, mature industries will accommodate it through further incremental adaptation; where substantial, they are thrown back on a new learning process and thus brought face-to-face with the threat of de-maturity. It is our strong belief that, properly understood, the possibilities of a restored technology-based competition—that is, a mode of competition in which producers once again actively seek out distinctive technical solutions to the product attributes favored by the market—can turn the threat of de-maturity into an attractive program for industry renewal.

Chapter 3

*The American System
of Manufacturing*

TO SPEAK about the linkage between technology and competition is to acknowledge, but understate, the all-important means by which that linkage is
accomplished. Perturbations in a design hierarchy offer no immediate leverage
on competitive advantage, nor do they pose an immediate threat to established
modes of doing business. Unless and until those perturbations express themselves in a company's overall manufacturing competence, they are invisible
in terms relevant to the market. The skills, systems, and organizational resources that together comprise a production system are, in a word, the means
by which technical change becomes competitively visible.

Thus, no understanding of this linkage can be adequate, let alone complete,
that does not pay close attention to the work of management. Skills, systems,
and resources do not simply appear as needed, nor do meaningful technical
advances take place in an organizational vacuum. There must be responsible
individuals who identify and funnel effort toward some design concepts and
some approaches to manufacturing rather than others, who perceive relevant
connections between those concepts and market preferences, who scan developments in government, university, and industrial laboratories for evidence
of new technical means to address these preferences, and who distill the lessons
of cumulative production experience. And these individuals must also be responsible for turning such ideas and perceptions into real processes and prod-

ucts. People, equipment, and systems must be brought to bear on the appropriate opportunities, must be taught or designed to do the new jobs required of them, must be given sufficient support.

American industry has often paid dearly for the error of treating the management of technology and the management of production as if they were separate, often mutually exclusive activities. These activities cannot be followed independently—save at great, if not immediately obvious, cost to competitive vigor. Binding them together, however, does not mean specifying once-and-for-all what the key managerial tasks and responsibilities are. These will change as industries, technologies, and production systems evolve. And evolve they do.

No industry's production system, after all, has ever sprung into existence fully developed. Much as the manufacturing competence of an industry evolves—as chapter 2 suggests—in response to changes in products, processes, and markets, so the general competence of the nation as a whole has evolved over time. The practices and modes of organization being followed at any given moment are the cumulative product of both sequences of development. Thus, to understand the critical, managerially relevant linkages among production competence, technology, and competition, we need to know something about the general history of American manufacturing, as well as about the history of particular industries.[1]

Adopting this historical perspective is useful for two reasons. First, given the critical importance of management in determining how technology gets brought into the marketplace and what it means for competition, we want to keep in sharp focus the inherited constraints under which management labors. Established production systems are not flimsy structures built upon sand. They are deeply rooted, and their roots say much about how they can adjust to new competitive realities. Second, we want to keep equally in focus the notion that a production system's past course of development is not just a constraint but a resource as well. It is a repository of experience and expertise that can be tapped at need.

In the early nineteenth century, the managers responsible for building the American system of manufacturing addressed themselves to the extraordinary competitive opportunities made possible in their day by an unprecedented season of technological ferment. They did so with the tools and techniques that lay ready at hand. Once again, such a season is upon us, and once again the central managerial challenge is to bring manufacturing competence into line with altered terms of competition. Merely trying to imitate past successes is a course of action destined to fail, for the opportunities and dangers of the present are not simple repetitions of those of a century ago. However, we have much to learn from those earlier experiences by way of cumulative wisdom and by way of analogy.

II

Writing of the great stained glass windows at Chartres Cathedral, the American historian Henry Adams observed that the system of lighting "will have to remain a closed book because the feeling and experience which explained it once are lost, and we cannot recover either." Such is not the case, however, with the American system of manufacturing, for the art and experience that have gone into it are well known to the historical record. Indeed, that system, which crystallized during the mid-1800s and which for more than a century has powered the nation's industrial engine and earned the high regard of producers abroad, is anything but a closed book. Its animating principles lie open to inspection.

Inter-industry variations notwithstanding, the major stages through which the American system has passed represent the progressive redefinition over time of a coherent program for production. Because the development of standardized parts gave shape to much that was to follow, the most useful initial reference point from which to measure this shifting program is the state of light metalworking industries—firearms, clocks, watches, sewing machines, and the like—in southern New England during the early years of the nineteenth century.

When Eli Whitney, famed inventor of the cotton gin, took up a government contract in 1798 to deliver 10,000 complete stands of muskets two years later, the substandard quality of colonial manufacturing during the Revolutionary era was still fresh in the public mind. The last quarter of the eighteenth century had been dominated by small-scale cottage industries maintained largely by craftsmen and apprentices very much under the influence of European traditions of production. For many, the goal was as it had long been: to make custom-ordered, high-quality goods by means of assembly or crude hand manufacture—often with the use of imported parts. By the 1790s, however, the shortcomings of operations so structured could no longer be ignored.

In this craft-based system, the organization of tasks and procedures was, as a rule, markedly inefficient in its use of time and labor. Too much depended on the unique skills and the ofttimes capricious temperaments of master craftsmen, for production was structured not by functional specialization but by the older practice of one worker making an entire product by hand. Not surprisingly, finished products varied widely in quality and gross imperfections were common. There were simply not enough skilled crafts-men to go around, nor were the colonies or newly formed states rich enough in investment capital to offset the need for such craftsmen by purchasing available machinery.

Against this background, Whitney's approach to the manufacturing process stands out in sharp relief. Before starting on his government contract, he spent a year building the tools, jigs, and other production fixtures that would, taken together, make possible an ordered and integrated flow of work through his factory. At each station would be located the right numbers of tools, machines, parts, and skilled workmen to keep the flow of muskets steady. By organizing his factory so as to accommodate a regular process of manufacture and by building machinery capable of working within fine tolerances, Whitney rede-fined the nature of the production task. No longer was it to coordinate the efforts of individual virtuosos; now it was to solve the technical problems of process organization.

These advances, especially as refined by other armsmakers like John Hall, Simeon North, and Samuel Colt, left a clear mark on most areas of American manufacturing. The concept of progressive work flows placed the responsibil-ity for product quantity and quality on the internal coherence of the manufac-turing system—and not on the whims of individual craftsmen. Equally impor-tant, the on-site development of specialized machine tools made possible the consistent precision essential to the production and assembly of interchange-able parts. But neither the better organization of work nor the greater refine-ment of equipment translated directly into an improved system of production. Also present, if we are to believe contemporary observers, were the remarkable talents and abilities of the American worker.

According to the 1868 report of a British Parliamentary Committee, the American worker

readily produces a new article; he understands everything you say to him as well as a man from a college in England would; he helps the employer by his own acuteness and intelligence; and, in consequence, he readily attains to any new knowledge, greatly assisting his employer by thoroughly understanding what is the change that is needed, and helping him on the road towards it.[2]

Many European visitors during the mid-nineteenth century noted the relation among better transportation systems, consumer acceptance of low-priced mass-produced goods, and the stunning growth of the American economy. But all who looked closely were more forcefully struck by the absence in American factories of the organizational rigidities so familiar in the European, by the concern of workers for personal advancement and material welfare, and by the belief of workers and managers alike in the boundless adaptability of American labor.[3]

III

The first stage of the American manufacturing system, then, witnessed the development of factories well suited to the sequential production of simple, imitative, and not very capital-intensive products which were assembled from machine-made and largely interchangeable parts. Although these advances reduced costs while boosting both output and quality, managers had not yet learned how to balance the emerging requirements of process standardization against the market's need for product variety and change. No staff was allocated to the work of introducing new product technology on a systematic basis, for the economic appeal of such introductions was minimal. Any major changeover would bring operations to a halt while new tools were fabricated and process flows restructured. As a result, during the first fifty years of the production in quantity of shelf clocks, to take but one example, only six different varieties (the variation lying mostly in choice of material, not in design) emerged from American clock factories.

Here matters stood until increasing demand for volume production of consumer goods like sewing machines helped push domestic factories into the second stage of development. To accommodate these higher volumes, products had to be broken down into clusters of technologically specialized components and the components assigned to different factory work units, which would feed them at need into the overall process flow. This arrangement, in turn, tended to give the individual work units an unprecedented degree of freedom. As Alfred Chandler has noted with specific reference to the metalworking industries,

[manufacturers] turned the day-to-day operations of the new factories over to the foremen of the several departments. As in the case of the iron and steel mills, these foremen controlled; they hired, fired, and promoted their working force. In those departments requiring the most intricate processing techniques in grinding, polishing, and other finishing of metal components, the foremen were responsible for the profitability as well as the productivity of their departments.[4]

In many respects, the sewing machine company of Isaac M. Singer pioneered this second stage of development: building a manufacturing organization flexible enough to assimilate technological advances while offering substantial product variety at low cost and at uniformly high levels of quality. As one 1880 publication reported,

the Singer Company makes no second grade articles, and puts nothing but the very best material and workmanship into any of its machines, finding, by experience, that it pays to put just as good parts into its cheapest as into its highest priced pearled and ornamented cabinet machine. Indeed, the only difference between the cheapest genuine Singer and the most costly machine is in the finish, decorations, and cabinet work. All the working parts are exactly the same.[5]

The basis of Singer's accomplishment? Quite simply, the use of families of specialized and standardized technological components, the application of time and energy to product design, and the careful organization of the production system as a vertically integrated whole. In fact, the thirty-two-acre plant built by the company in 1873 had its own rail-supplied foundry, forging shop, milling department, and multiple facilities for the inspection and testing both of components and final products. Coupled with aggressive marketing techniques (agents and canvassers, retail outlets, credit and installment buying programs, and a huge advertising budget), these second-stage advances in manufacturing permitted Singer by the late 1870s to dominate three-quarters of the world market for sewing machines. At the same time, of course, it was the existence of such mass markets—themselves made possible by great improvements in transportation and communication—that created the environment within which second-stage activities made sense and could flourish.

Other companies shared in Singer's pathbreaking efforts, but many still fell into a troubling pattern of manufacturing a product with increasing efficiency until the product itself became obsolete. Without an in-house commitment to making systematic product line improvement a focus of competitive energy, these companies literally ran their operations into the ground and ultimately had to either sell out to a competitor or go out of business entirely.

By contrast, Samuel Colt, the legendary armsmaker, and his production expert Elisha K. Root confronted these issues directly. Not only did they employ the very latest in production equipment and technique; they also took American manufacturing into its third stage by institutionalizing constant improvements in process and product technology as a deliberately chosen means for achieving competitive advantage. In the words of British manufacturers who toured the United States in 1853,

It is Colonel Colt's intention, the committee understands, to manufacture in large quantities two different sizes of revolving rifles. . . . The pattern proposed was not complete, but was shown to the committee. In principle it was the same as the Colt pistol, but in detail varied considerably from that weapon. Colonel Colt has also a new pattern pistol, very small indeed, which he intends making in large quantities, at very low cost.[6]

Colt's sensitivity to—and emphasis on—planned product change, new product development, and an up-to-date manufacturing plant brought American production into its third phase of development. Even so, the immense practical difficulties in managing vertically integrated facilities during a period of rapid technological change just as rapidly made such third-stage achievements incomplete. Missing still was a coherent and reliable set of relations between manufacturers and technology-based suppliers of components.

IV

In retrospect, it is clear that American companies were relatively quick to adapt to the central reality of fourth-stage development: the new-found importance of suppliers. As one historian comments, "American firms showed a much greater talent than British firms for coordinating successfully their relationships with other firms upon whom they were dependent for the supply of essential inputs."[7] At the end of the nineteenth century, for example, the largest bicycle and carriage makers—firms like Pope Manufacturing and Durant-Dort Carriage—handled most of their parts requirements in-house, but they had already begun to rely on outside suppliers for the development of certain technologically advanced components. Small and medium-sized firms, however, routinely turned to suppliers for such basic items as tires, wheels, seat pillars, and ball bearings.

The logic here was simple. External sourcing allowed manufacturers to acquire needed components at a far lower cost than if they had had to pay for specialized tooling and development work themselves. By avoiding the substantial investments in capital equipment and design personnel necessary to component fabrication and by sharing in the scale economies enjoyed by specialized parts makers, manufacturers hit upon a relatively inexpensive way of keeping themselves at the cutting edge of technical progress. But at a price.

Not surprisingly, as the sophistication of what suppliers did increased, the range of components each was able to offer decreased; and this, in turn, forced producers to establish relationships with a number of different suppliers. Managing these relationships in an effective and timely fashion demanded a whole new level of organizational competence at precisely the same time that the penalty for incompetence was growing ever more serious. Reliance on suppliers might facilitate low cost access to new technology, but it made producers vulnerable in a way they had not been before. As Chandler pointedly remarks, "a manufacturer could not risk having to stop his whole production line merely because a supplier had been unable to deliver spark plugs, flywheels, or roller bearings at the promised time."[8]

These fourth-stage developments—the most advanced expressions of American manufacturing at the end of the nineteenth century—are of interest for yet another reason. The rapid proliferation during these years of machine shops, die makers, and technology-based suppliers helped prepare the ground for the first generation of automobile manufacturing. Because the needs of bicycle and carriagemakers had fostered the crazy-quilt evolution of an industrial infrastructure, early makers of automobiles were, for the most part, assemblers who put together in rented shops components supplied by others. Assemblers though they were, their efforts rested on a, by then, well developed and widely diffused competence in manufacturing. Only because a host of other shops and companies had mastered the full range of skills, technical and organizational, pioneered during the nineteenth century, could the first generation of work on automobiles get anywhere.

Many early producers—Duryea, Winton, Durant, the Dodges, and the Studebakers, among others—had their roots in bicycle or carriage manufacturing. Henry Leland, who supplied engines to Ford as well as the Olds Motor Works before forming the Cadillac Motor Car Company in 1902, had worked years before in the revolver factory of Samuel Colt and then established his own machine shop. This kind of personal experience with process technology and sourced components—no less than the existence of a supplier infrastructure—was an essential precondition for the twentieth-century development of technically advanced manufacturing industry. Of Leland's shop, for example, Allan Nevins reports,

To work to a 1/10,000 of an inch was not exceptional in that factory, and Henry M. Leland could supervise production requiring 1/1,000,000 of an inch. The firm had devised or improved some of the machine tools and had worked out the revolutionary methods which produced the gears for the Columbia bicycle and other metal products combining great delicacy, strength, and precision.[9]

Especially during a period of great technological ferment like that which characterized the first few decades of the automobile industry, skills on the order of Leland's are invaluable to competitive success. Building and running production systems that can accommodate the latest technical wrinkle are precisely what the business is all about.

Management competence is, of course, the medium through which these skills get translated into terms relevant to the market, but in the early stages of industry—even fourth-stage industry—development, it is not so important as it will later become. What a man can do in his own garage or workshop can still have a direct effect on the progress of design concepts, the structure of operations, and the nature of competition. True, the seemingly infinite flexibility that typified the cottage industries of the eighteenth century had disappeared forever by the time automobile producers began their work in earnest, but the world in which they labored was sufficiently open-ended, sufficiently immediate in its linkage of technology with the market, that something of that older flexibility remained.

Not only, then, is the automobile industry broadly representative of manufacturing industries generally; it stands as the historical culmination of the American manufacturing system itself. Building automobiles has, from the outset, called on the full range of American production competence. Thus, both as a symbol and as an industry specific to a given historical place and time, automobile manufacturing is the legitimate capstone of the American system.

V

At each of these stages of the American system's evolution, the tell-tale managerial accomplishment was to develop ever more sophisticated forms of institutional mechanisms for harnessing new technical possibilities to the work of production. By itself, neither skill in innovation nor skill in manufacturing was enough. From Whitney's day onward, the challenge has been to master both. Not surprisingly, then, to be able to produce technologically complex products at high volume was the last major development needed to bring that system into recognizably modern shape. The automobile producers, led by Ford, relied on new technology and new systems of management to control the smooth and unbroken flow of products through their various stages of fabrication and assembly. Indeed, the mastery of a genuine "flow" system of production at high-volume levels defined the organizational competence on which would rest the great manufacturing achievements of twentieth-century American industry.

When we think of the salad days of the nation's industrial plant during and after World War II, it is this fifth-stage incarnation of the American system that comes to mind. The principles of this stage have received some attention in the previous chapter and will receive more detailed treatment in the chapters to follow. Here we want only to note that so powerful was this managerial achievement, so successful the response awarded it in the marketplace, so huge the industry's size, and so influential its effects on other industries that automobile production became the model of choice for American manufacturing. By the sheer force of its example, Detroit pulled the nation's manufacturing base toward its own fifth-stage image of development.

Despite their many advances in the organization of production, the operations of Colt and Singer were designed to take advantage of the distinct processing capabilities of focused areas within their factories. As a result, production equipment was grouped according to the nature of the operation performed. Workmen had to convey material in the process of manufacture from one cluster of equipment to another as the sequence of production tasks determined, and this requirement led in turn both to much backtracking and crisscrossing in the flow of material and to the building up of excessive levels of inventory.

No small part of Henry Ford's accomplishment, therefore, was his ruthless and tireless insistence on the overall rationalization of the manufacturing system. By organizing operations at Highland Park strictly in terms of the necessary flow of work, by using separate production lines for each component to reduce process bottlenecks, by applying conveyors and other techniques of line-flow management, and by driving inventories down to the lowest acceptable level, Ford did much to perfect the fifth-stage arrangement of production. True, Ford managers and even Ford himself were acutely aware that they had not solved what they called their "labor problem"—that is, the integration of the work force into the production process not as a faceless mechanism but as a reservoir of competitively valuable human strengths. But commercial success diminished the urgency of the problem.

That success, however, created additional problems. Booming demand for Ford cars led the company to decentralize assembly operations—first in Kansas City, Missouri, in 1910 and then in a total of some thirty different locations. How to manage in a cost-effective way the timely supply of parts to these geographically separate facilities? Ford addressed the logistics of decentralization by having suppliers ship directly to the assembly plants and by establishing, where possible, sources of supply close to the plant sites.

Single-minded rationalization of production and coordination of multi-plant operations completed the development of the American system as we have known it. Refinements would, of course, occur, but all the essential pieces were now in place to support the heydey of modern American industry. This was the manufacturing plant that won the second World War, that drove the greatest era of sustained prosperity in recent history, and that—in terms of the automobile industry proper, that preeminent feature of the nation's economic land-

39

scape—efficiently produced the all-purpose roadcruiser, which controlled the market for thirty years.

With the roadcruiser and the production base responsible for building it, American industry had at last achieved unquestioned dominance in the work of manufacturing. Or had it? Industry certainly thought so, for the next several decades were to see a redirection of managerial effort and attention away from production and toward marketing and finance. After all, the age-old "problem of production" had been solved, and the task at hand was now to seek out greener pastures for managerial effort. But there were other managers, in countries other than the United States, who were not so sure. Perhaps better training and more creative integration of a skilled labor force into the production process could open up a sixth stage, much as such efforts have already opened up a sixth stage in Japanese manufacturing. Perhaps there were yet further stages to be reached by diligent and relentless concentration on the joint mastery of technology and production.

The comfortable maturity into which American automobile makers drifted during the 1950s and 1960s kept all such potentially disquieting questions at bay. Like their counterparts in other manufacturing industries, executives in Detroit felt they had found the key to unlock forever the bounties of a secure domestic market. Their confidence was soon to cost them dearly.

PART II

The Case of the Automobile Industry

HOW is it possible that U.S. and Japanese manufacturers can vary so greatly in their mastery of the tasks essential to building a product like the automobile? The production systems on which they rely are not some rootless construction of the moment; they are, on the contrary, the capstone of long sequences of manufacturing history and reflect the accumulated wisdom and experience of many industries. How can these systems for doing precisely the same kinds of things provide the leverage for overwhelming competitive advantage?

Any close inspection of the U.S. automobile industry must take questions like these seriously, for they pose directly the central challenge that now faces American managers. When similarity of production experience does not guarantee similarity of result, where can the source of the difference lie if not—in large measure, at least—in the efforts of management to integrate equipment, systems, and the people who run them into a company's overall strategic purposes? Where else can improvement be found if not in the ability of management to focus organizational skills, energies, and resources by bringing production competence to bear on the key points of competitive leverage?

We turn in the next four chapters to a detailed study of the work of building automobiles because that study offers an exceptionally rich opportunity to understand what it takes in today's environment to develop and employ production competence as a formidable competitive asset. Equally important, we shall also see what happens when that competence is neither so developed nor so employed.

Chapter 4

Internationalization and the Challenge of New Competitors, Products, and Technology

FOR the U.S. automobile industry, the past decade has been a time of crisis and transition. The turmoil in which domestic producers have found themselves does not represent a continuation of business as usual with the simple addition of a new cast of characters. It reflects, instead, a fundamental change in the basis of industry competition—the onset, to return to the concept developed in chapter 2, of de-maturity. The immediate sources of this change are not difficult to identify: rising oil prices, vigorous foreign competitors, and shifts in market demand. Less obvious are the reasons why industry adjustments have taken the precise form they have. In large measure, the industry has adapted to de-maturity in the way it has because of the course it followed throughout this century as it evolved into modern form. Detroit's history has constrained its present actions.

When Henry Ford began to tinker with the idea of making an automobile, the industry (if one could call it that) was young and its future direction ill-defined. Dozens of budding entrepreneurs labored in sheds, small shops, and garages to turn out a bewildering variety of what they called automobiles.

There were cars powered by electricity, steam, and gasoline; cars with three wheels and four; cars with a wheel for steering and cars with a tiller. Technological uncertainty reigned among producers and buyers alike. No one knew for sure what buyers' preferences would be or what technologies would be best able to meet them.

As search and learning behavior proceeded on both sides of the market, some concepts won general acceptance—internal combustion engines fueled by gasoline, for example, and front-mounted engines, direct drive shafts, and left-handed steering. In 1908 Henry Ford synthesized these concepts into an overall design, the Model T, that was to dominate the industry for fifteen years. Ford's view of the automobile as a low-priced, durable, and reliable means of basic transportation opened the way for the development of a mass market for automobiles and, in so doing, transformed the industry. If, in 1908, the work of production was not far removed from the small shop or garage, by 1915 it had already evolved toward the large, capital-intensive, and highly integrated factories of a mass production industry. The sheer size and complexity of these operations and of the organizations needed to control them gave rise to what Alfred Chandler has called "giant enterprise." Equally important, this enlarged scale of operations turned what had been competition among a multitude of small firms into a contest among a few large ones.

The enormous success of the Model T gave Ford a commanding position in the rapidly expanding market of the 1910s, but the Tin Lizzie's appeal as rugged basic transportation began to wane as new technologies—like the closed steel body—and shifting market preferences created a demand for improved comfort, convenience, and ease of operation. Ford's response was to cut prices and to offer modest design changes, but these gestures were not enough to satisfy consumers, whose sense of what they wanted a car to be had substantially altered. GM understood in a way Ford did not that the public wanted (and new technology had begun to make possible) greater interior comfort, style, luxury, and smoothness of ride. The automobile was no longer to be, first and foremost, a rural utility vehicle; it was now to be something closer to a "living room on wheels."

This redefinition of the automobile established a whole new agenda for technical innovation. True, the ferment in markets and technology did not during the 1920s and 1930s reach far enough into the design hierarchy to displace basic core concepts in mechanics or structure, but it did create incentives for active exploration of new ideas in suspensions, transmissions, engines, and car bodies. This exploration, in turn, marked a reversal in the pattern of industry development. What emerged from this limited phase of de-maturity was a general convergence on the design of the all-purpose roadcruiser—front-mounted, water-cooled, V-8 gasoline engine; rear wheel drive;

automatic transmission—that would dominate the industry for three decades.

During the 1930s GM led the movement toward the road cruiser's technical configuration, but by 1940—with that design firmly locked into place—the industry's competitive agenda shifted away from innovative effort. A decade later, after the upheavals of wartime production, the industry had developed virtually all the tell-tale signs of maturity: the small producers that had once populated its periphery had either merged or disappeared altogether; the few large firms that remained competed with each other on the basis of styling, dealer service, and economies of scale in production; product technology had become standardized; and the manufacturing process had been embodied in the capital equipment generally available for sale.

In competitive terms, the postwar domestic industry was self-contained. Rivalry was a matter of what GM was up to, what Ford's plans were, how Chrysler would react. And why not, since the size of the domestic market dwarfed all other markets. In 1955, for example, nearly 80 percent of all new car registrations in the world occurred in the United States. Detroit was not only the home of the giant U.S. firms; it was the hub of the automotive universe. Or so it must have seemed. Throughout the 1950s, developments in Europe no doubt had the quality of small skirmishes out somewhere on the industry's borders; developments in Japan, which produced all of 4,000 cars in 1955, were of no significance at all. The real action was at home.

And that action was heady stuff. The market for automobiles after World War II was a seller's market, and the domestic producers flourished. Increases in costs were readily passed along to the consumer, whose appetite for fins, chrome, and horsepower appeared insatiable. Success bred success and confirmed the managerial decisions responsible for it. Some foreign producers—notably Volkswagen—had begun to nibble away at the very low end of the market, but this did not seem a major threat. In retrospect, of course, we can see that what looked in the mid-1950s like the minor inroads of pesky foreigners was in fact the beginning of a profound change in the domestic market—and of a vigorous competitive challenge from abroad.

II

The international trade in automobiles, which has come to loom so large on Detroit's horizons, never amounted to much during the industry's early years. Before World War I, for example, the American market was both protected from imports by a 45 percent ad valorem tariff and discouraged from exporting by high transportation costs.[1] Even though European governments initially set low tariff barriers (in 1911–1912 the British had none at all), they quickly adopted protectionist measures when those transportation costs fell and competition increased. The British instituted a 33½ percent tariff in 1915; the French, one of 45 percent in 1922, which they raised to 90 percent in 1931; the Germans, a mixture of tariffs, taxes based on engine displacement, foreign exchange regulations, and local content requirements. The implication of these actions was not lost on the Americans, and by 1929 Ford and GM had either established or acquired a total of sixty-eight production facilities in Europe.

On the eve of World War II, therefore, direct international trade in automobiles was insignificant. The various European and Japanese producers sat behind one or another sort of government protection, and the Americans were shielded from international trade by the particular nature of the then domestic market. The need to set up extensive dealer and service networks made import penetration difficult, as did the preference of most drivers for comfortable, reliable, general-purpose vehicles that were easy to operate and maintain. The U.S. market was a mass market and showed a pronounced aversion to technical features like precision gearshifting that required substantial driver skill. In Europe, by contrast, sophisticated consumers placed a high premium on performance, and taxes on gasoline and horsepower pushed technical advances in engines and fuel economy that had little, if any, appeal to the American market.

After the war, changing consumer preferences in the United States and the formation of the EEC (European Economic Community) prompted much higher levels of trade. French, German, and Italian producers capitalized on the dismantling of trade barriers to build strong positions throughout Europe; Volkswagen, as already noted, established a beachhead in the U.S. market. From these beginnings, the growth of trade during the 1960s was striking. Between 1955 and 1970, for example, the ratio of imports to the total world production of automobiles rose from 1.8 percent to 20.2 percent, the rise being greatest in the United States.[2] By 1970 a full 15 percent of domestic car sales were imports, mostly German.

More recently, the oil shocks of 1973 and 1979 accentuated these earlier trends, but with an emphasis on worldwide exports by the Japanese. In the United States, for example, total demand for automobiles increased by 30 percent between 1970 and 1980, but the demand for Japanese cars grew fivefold to a level of nearly two million vehicles a year by the end of that period. Nor was the Japanese success limited to the American market: Britain, the Benelux countries, and West Germany also proved receptive. As late as 1978 German auto executives thought the German market's preference for high performance, engineering, and quality made tariffs and import quotas unnecessary. By 1980, however, as Japanese penetration passed 9 percent, those executives had rather abruptly changed their tune.

The continuing export thrust of the Europeans, the emergence of the Japanese as world-class competitors (with some help, we should note, from trade barriers erected by the Japanese government to protect its own domestic market), the growing interdependence of the world market for automobiles, the appearance of production bases in such developing nations as Mexico and Brazil, and the slow convergence of American consumers' demands with those of consumers abroad—taken together, these trade-related developments have given the U.S. industry a distinctly international, not just multinational, cast. And this process of internationalization has, in turn, profoundly influenced both the competitive structure of the world industry and the competitive strategies of its major participants.

One useful way of visualizing this move toward internationalization is to chart over time the growth in the number of equivalent firms in the industry worldwide. Roughly speaking, this is a measure of the number of firms that would populate an industry if all participants had the same share of the market as did the larger firms.[3] A rise in this index, therefore, is an indication that market power is becoming less concentrated. As figure 4.1 indicates, during the mid-1950s world industry was populated by only five equivalent firms. GM, Ford, and Chrysler were the dominant forces, and everyone else—Renault, Peugeot, Mercedes, Toyota, Nissan, and the rest—accounted for only two additional firms of comparable size. By the late 1960s, however, the growth of European producers had made substantial inroads into the market share of U.S. manufacturers and had boosted the number of equivalent firms to eight. During the 1970s, the explosive boom in Japanese exports—coupled with a strong domestic market in Japan—pushed that number to ten. Thus, although there have been year-to-year fluctuations, the inescapable fact is that over the past quarter century, the number of equivalent firms has doubled.

The realities of internationalization have made themselves felt in a variety of ways. Consider, for example, the production of what has come to be called the "world car." The competitive forces unleashed by the internationalization of the world industry in the late 1950s and 1960s gave new life to the idea of designing a car for several national markets and building it from a multinational production base. These forces took root most firmly in Europe, where the breakdown of small-scale production aimed at single national markets accelerated in the 1960s. In fact, several firms—Ford, GM, and VW among them—have sought to integrate their various European operations into a single coherent entity. By rationalizing design and production processes across na-

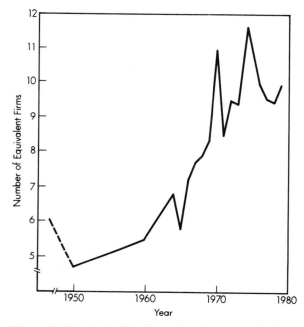

Figure 4.1 *Trends in World Automobile Market Structure*

SOURCE: Beginning to 1965: Raymond Vernon *Storm Over the Multinationals: The Real Issue* (Cambridge: Harvard University, 1977). 1965 to 1979: Calculated from data in *World Motor Vehicle Data* (Detroit: Motor Vehicle Manufacturers Association, 1980).

NOTE: The number of "equivalent firms" is calculated as defined in the text.

tional markets, standardizing components across models, and centralizing the production of components to take advantage of scale economies, they hoped to become more efficient producers.[4]

In the aftermath of the oil shocks of the 1970s, several U.S. producers thought to extend this European strategy of integration beyond the multinational to a truly worldwide scale. In practice, however, although Ford and GM have developed cars (the Escort and the "J" cars) for both European and American markets, the different versions share only a similar shape and some components. They are world cars in name only. True, there has been movement toward global integration of component production in response to costs and to various local content requirements. But differences in regulation and consumer demand among the various national markets have, along with sheer organizational inertia, so far presented obstacles to full rationalization of automobile design and production.

Much the same considerations have given new impetus to alliances and coalitions among automobile manufacturers. Indeed, every major producer in the world has turned to one or another form of joint venture to achieve economies of scale, access to markets or new technology, or as a means of circumventing protectionist legislation.[5] Such alliances, of course, are nothing new, but their number, size, and scope have escalated dramatically during the past decade. At the same time, their form and purpose have changed. In the 1950s, for example, mergers and buyouts were common in the United States and Europe (especially Britain); since then, however, joint ventures and minority equity participations have tended to dominate. In the mid- to late 1960s, alliances were largely motivated by scale economies in either production or distribution; more recently, they have been driven by the desire for access to markets and technology. Honda's joint venture in Britain and Nissan's in Italy, to take but two obvious cases, seem designed to finesse actual or potential trade restrictions.

What have been the most lasting effects of such arrangements and, more broadly, of the internationalization they represent on the automobile industry's structure and dynamics of competition? As we explain in some detail in appendix A, as an industry evolves, the number, strength, and relative size of its competitors shift in a roughly predictable fashion to accommodate the changing interactions of market growth and technological innovation. It is against such a backdrop as this that the various aspects of internationalization take on competitive significance.

Some alliances may, for example, actually reduce the effective number of participants; others may turn their members into more vigorous competitors. Firms that cooperate in the production of engines, say, may differentiate their products in countless other ways. The V-6 engines that Citroën manufactures at the new Dovrin plant, which it shares with Volvo and Renault, have strengthened its hand in the luxury car market—much to Volvo's dismay. On balance, then, joint ventures have no invariable effect on competition. They might help sustain a larger number of independent producers than might otherwise survive. They could also, however, be the prelude to a merger or to some form of cartel-like behavior and thus help weaken competition.

With alliances and joint ventures, as with other aspects of the industry's internationalization, the relevant measure of the character of competition is not a simple calculation of market share but a careful determination at a given point in time of the precise relationships among market preference, technical configuration, and competitive focus. Nowhere is this truth more forcefully illustrated than in the long-term decline of the relative market positions of GM, Ford, and Chrysler. (Again, see figure 4.1.) In retrospect, however, it is clear that the emergence of strong, world-class foreign competitors was significant not so much because domestic firms lost market share as because the new players changed the nature, scale, and complexity of industry competition. Beginning in the late 1950s and greatly accelerated by the events of the 1970s, internationalization redefined what it took to be a successful automobile producer. Conventional wisdom and past practice no longer applied. The lessons of an industrial lifetime had to be unlearned.

III

What the growth of foreign-based competition actually meant for Detroit can be most clearly seen in the saga of the small car in the U.S. market.[6] Although they have been a major fact of life in the industry's development in most countries, small cars occupied a rather specialized niche in the U.S. market until the late 1970s—a niche served primarily by foreign producers. By virtue of the kind of production technology and domestic competition that emerged during the 1920s, American manufacturers were unable to achieve sufficient economies in materials, design, or production to offer a low-priced small car that returned a decent profit, given the U.S. market's demonstrated preference for large cars. As one of Detroit's favorite generalizations of the 1950s had it, "small car, small profits."

This poor record was not for lack of trying. In 1907 Alanson Brush offered the 500 Brush Runabout, which featured replaceable wooden axles and frames as a means of reducing cost.[7] During the Great Depression of the 1930s, a number of producers—Graham, Reo, and Hupmobile among them—made an early stab at downsizing. Just before World War II, Powell Crosley, Jr., introduced an all-new small car, the Crosley. None of these efforts enjoyed much success, for the Brush Runabout proved undependable, and the introduction of closed steel bodies during the 1920s pushed the industry's dominant design and market structure in a different direction.

In practice, the arrival of closed steel bodies worked a major change in the concept of the automobile and established a whole new set of criteria for automobile design: passenger comfort, room, heating, ventilation, and smoothness and quietness of ride. The larger-sized cars that made these amenities possible were particularly well suited to the geographical expanse of the United States and to the substantial distances that its drivers had to cover. Moreover, especially in the days before regular airplane travel and before the easy availability of rental equipment for moving physical goods, the larger-sized car also served as a surrogate truck and family recreational vehicle. These developments suited domestic producers quite well because increasing size and weight—given the realities of automobile manufacture—meant enhanced opportunities for profit.

As the industry evolved toward the all-purpose roadcruiser of the late 1940s, market preferences and the dynamics of production helped to define the industry's basis of competition in terms of product-line strategy—that is, in terms of meeting market needs through adjustments in an entire product line and not through independent variations in technology or design. Good product policy meant a rational distribution of models by size and price, and the market's association of larger size and greater expense with luxury and comfort made possible an eminently "rational" set of relationships between a vehicle's weight and the price the market was willing to pay for it. Indeed, as automobiles grew larger, that relationship became progressively stronger.

Figure 4.2 documents, by way of example, the extraordinary smoothness of the industry's price/weight relationship for the period 1958–1960. Figure 4.2 also shows, however, the very different curve graphed by the relationship between weight and cost. Over the range of most model sizes, production costs simply did not grow as rapidly as did market prices with increases in vehicle weight. As a result, relatively narrow price/cost margins (the area between the two curves) characterized the small car segment of the industry; at the other end, of course, the margins were immense.

The facts of competitive life represented by this juxtaposition of curves are not some recent vagary of the postwar era. They are inextricably connected with the way the industry developed in America. By 1936, no major U.S. producer was making cars for the low-price segment of the market that had been served by the Model T. This is no cause for surprise. Given the nature of the search for acceptable technical configurations, the appearance of core concepts and dominant designs, and the economies of scale in production, profits lay elsewhere. Nor ought there be any surprise that, when Ford built a small car—the 92A—to serve the Model T's old segment of the market, it was an economic failure although a technical success.

Eugene Farkas of Ford's engine development group based the 92A on a 136-cubic-inch displacement version of the V-8 engine, which was first introduced to the market in 1932, and on a scaled-down version of the standard Ford frame and body. Allan Nevins provides a succinct account of the 92A's failure:

Farkas. . . used the smaller V-8 engine, and the 92A, as the car was called, emerged narrower and shorter than the regular Ford, and 600 pounds lighter. The first completed model, as Farkas recalls, was a "sweet running job." But difficulties arose. The

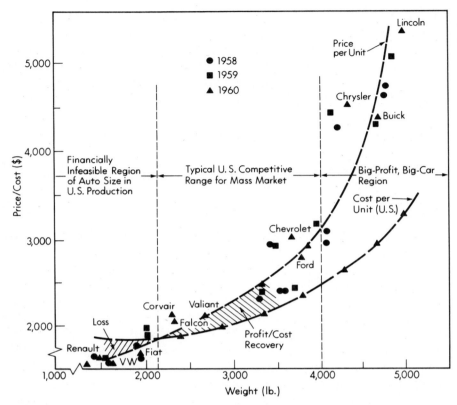

Figure 4.2 *Price, Cost, and Vehicle Size for Selected Models: 1958, 1959, and 1960*

SOURCE: *Consumer Reports,* April issues, 1958–1960.

NOTE: The price curve is based on actual list prices of selected models; the cost curve is representative; it is based on general information about the relative cost of cars by weight.

small motor cost but $3 less to manufacture than the larger one. Wibel calculated the possible savings in each case at a mere $36. Since the 92A would have to compete with year-old larger used cars, this was not enough. . . so by mid April the project was abandoned. . .[8]

Ford discovered that it took about as much time to fasten a small bolt as a large one, about as much working capital to finance and as much effort to transport a small engine block as a large one, and so on. Little of the cost of production depended on the size or weight of the 92A's adapted components—save, perhaps, for their slightly lower material content. True cost reduction would come, if at all, only if Ford were to design the car over from scratch and establish new facilities dedicated to its production. But given the clear preference of the market for larger cars and the huge expense of tooling up to make a replacement for the Model T, Ford could neither justify the capital outlay nor make a worthwhile profit on a jerrybuilt 92A.

The logic that led Ford to abandon this project dominated the thinking of all major U.S. producers in the years after World War II. That they listened to it was neither foolish nor foolhardy. True, it left the small car market unguarded, the Achilles heel of the industry, but it was at the time a perfectly reasonable response to the nature of competition in that industry. For foreign producers like Volkswagen and Renault, however, it left an opening, and they based their assault on the low end of the U.S. market on price, quality, and economy of operation. By 1959, imports such as these had taken a full 10 percent of the domestic market. Taken together, imports and the small cars produced by the second tier of U.S. firms (American Motors and Studebaker) accounted for 18.4 percent of the market.

For this activity in the small car segment, the major producers were not entirely unprepared. They had in the past addressed that segment by importing products from their European subsidiaries, and in the fall of 1959 they introduced products of their own: the Corvair, Falcon, and Valiant. These new compact models, as they were called, were indeed smaller than the standard American sedans, but they were also larger, heavier, and more expensive than their import competition. Following the classic GM marketing strategy developed by Alfred Sloan for use against Ford, the domestic manufacturers sought to define and fill a segment of the market just a cut above that served by the imports and, of course, to charge a premium for their efforts. And they were successful. Sales of American-made compacts came, to some extent, at the expense of full-sized models and captive imports, but they were substantial enough to beat back the import challenge from foreign producers like Renault.

Sales of the VW Beetle, however, continued to grow. Its unusually low price made it quite attractive to domestic consumers, but so did the quality of its construction and performance. At the same time (1960) that *Consumer Reports* was chiding Corvair for its "unimpressive trim quality" and Valiant for its "poor finish," it was extolling VW's workmanship. Not only that, changing market preferences found the "Bug" fun to drive. As *Consumer Reports* noted, the Bug's "handling and roadability are well ahead of the U.S. average."[9] Volkswagen had done its homework well and understood that low price and high quality could force an entry into the U.S. market—but only if they were supported with a competent sales and service network. This VW took pains to establish, and the strategy paid off in booming sales.

Throughout this period domestic producers toyed with the possibility of meeting the small imports head-on instead of trying to outflank them with compacts. In fact, before the compacts had proven themselves in the market, Ford had begun development of a car, code-named the Cardinal, with a

96-inch wheelbase, front-wheel drive, and a front-mounted, four-cylinder engine.[10] Although the Cardinal was produced in West Germany as the Taunus 12M, Ford decided not to build it in the United States. The reason for Ford's retreat is simply put: at the time of the Cardinal's scheduled introduction in 1962, imports had slipped back to 5 percent of the market, and there was growing evidence that consumers were eager—if given the chance—to trade up to larger, more luxurious versions of the compact models. This was evidence of a sort that Ford managers wanted to believe, for it allowed them to keep operating within familiar competitive boundaries. Unfortunately, of course, the reduced demand for imports was to prove temporary, for the forces that drove that demand reflected fundamental demographic trends (increased suburbanization, shifts in the age structure of the driving population, changes in labor-force participation by women, growth in the number of multi-car families, and so on) that would not disappear merely because they were inconvenient.

In retrospect, then, we can see that Detroit's early flirtation with a new calculus of automobile design and production was at base a continuation of past practice, a somewhat half-hearted attempt to view the competitive dynamics of the industry in different terms. Just how strong a grip the logic of large car production had on the industry can be seen in the compacts' steady increase in size and weight during the years they were in production. Indeed, each year seemed to bring a few more inches and a few more pounds until, by the late 1960s, even a once trim car like the Falcon had added a foot in length and 500 pounds in weight. Detroit, in effect, first tried to build small cars by making little big cars.

But as import penetration reached and passed previous levels (in the early 1970s imports accounted for 15 percent of the market), Detroit finally acknowledged the need to get into the small car business in a serious way. Even so, its first offerings—the Vega, Pinto, and Gremlin—were heavier and had larger engines than their foreign competition. Unlike the compacts, however, and unlike Ford's experimentation with the 92A, these new subcompacts, as they were known, had been redesigned to change the established connections between cost and size in automobile production. The subcompacts not only had lower material requirements; they also used many fewer parts (a reduction of some 30 percent) and could be produced in a more highly automated fashion than the standard American sedan.

The events of the 1970s have been the catalyst for finally convincing managers in Detroit that the nature of the industry has changed. A market that had once been oriented toward smoothness of ride, passenger comfort, luxury, quiet, and large size has been transformed into a market concerned about efficient use of space and fuel, quality of construction, and reliability of operation

55

in cars of all sizes. So great are the implications of this shift for established design concepts and technologies that market preferences cannot be met through downsizing or other such adjustments but only through new technical concepts and new manufacturing objectives.

The automobile in demand in the early 1980s is, in an important sense, not an extension or refinement of the all-purpose roadcruiser of past decades but a different product altogether. True, it still has four wheels, an engine, and a steering wheel, but the guts of the car—its materials, engine, electronics, and the like—have changed dramatically. So, too, has the ground on which the industry competes. What a producer needs to be good at today is not at all what that producer needed to be good at two decades ago. Fueled by the internationalization of the industry, evolving market preferences have radically altered long-established relationships among price, cost, and size. They have also reopened the technical solutions that worked so well while those old relationships held. And, finally, by removing the shaping influence of familiar production economies and technological imperatives, they have thrown the structure of the industry into turmoil.

Detroit may still be home for the American automobile industry, but the inescapable realities of the new industrial competition have changed the very definition of home. Detroit is no longer the hub of the automotive universe, sufficient unto itself, and isolated from the world. It is now an outpost, albeit a very important one, of a worldwide industry, and its true horizons are measured not by domestic geography but, rather, by its ability to achieve excellence in the management of both technological innovation and production.

Chapter 5

Productivity, Cost, and Quality

THE EFFECTS of internationalization have, at last, buffeted American automobile producers into a new kind of awareness about the nature of their industry. To the extent that industry remains domestic, it is domestic only in the sense that much of its production base and a good proportion of its markets fall within the territorial boundaries of the United States. In terms of product design, however, or component sourcing or the identity of competitors, the self-contained world that Detroit once bestrode like a colossus exists no longer. With their products, costs, and performance, ambitious European and Japanese producers have established the new terms of competition.

European involvement in the American market, particularly in its luxury and high-performance segments, has a long history. During the past decade, however, the major influence on the domestic market has been the appearance of Japanese compacts and subcompacts. Accordingly, it is against the performance of Japanese manufacturers that we here seek to measure the costs, quality, and productivity of U.S. producers. We do so with a certain sense of irony. While more than 20 percent of the cars sold in the United States now come from Japan, it is hard to remember that there was a time—not all that long ago—when Japanese imports were a complete failure.

The first cars exported by Toyota to the United States in 1957 were of such poor quality that the attractiveness of their low price could not offset their disturbing tendency to break down after only a few hours of freeway driving.[1] By the time Toyota and Nissan returned to the U.S. market in the mid-1960s, however, they had taken to heart the lesson of VW's earlier success: combine low price with much higher levels of performance and quality than that price might suggest. Indeed, they clearly saw that the value of cost advantages in production was not so much to allow the skimming off of fat profits as to permit much greater leverage on competitive advantage in product performance and quality. Well before the oil shock of 1979 helped double the market share of Japanese imports within two years, the American market had begun to respond quite favorably to the skills the Japanese producers had gone far toward mastering.

In part because of their own past success and in part because the import fiasco of 1957 tagged the Japanese with an image of fumbling incompetence, American producers have been slow to recognize the extent and, more important, the sources of the Japanese challenge. That Toyota or Nissan might have an advantage in lower wage rates was understood early on; that they might also have an edge in product quality or productivity was a realization that began to dawn only in 1979. Even then, however, many American observers were inclined to attribute that edge to cultural traits, government policy, domestic savings rates, or levels of capital investment. That it might have something to do with the guts, the nuts-and-bolts of running a manufacturing operation, was a realization that has not fully sunk in even yet.

Thus, when we look, as we do in this chapter, to the data on costs, wage rates, and overall efficiency in the use of resources in automobile production, we do so because such information is representative—if not precisely, then in general outline—of the recent experience of a variety of other repetitive manufacturing industries. These data tell us something, if only indirectly, about the degree to which American competence in manufacturing has proven equal to the new terms of competition. What we find is sobering in the extreme. No amount of hype in the media can rob these numbers of their harsh or startling implications. Although constant harping on the economic challenge that Japan now presents to the West tends to numb the mind, to make us feel that when we have admitted the fact we have done enough, a close exposure to the inner mechanics of that challenge is like a splash of cold water. This is scary stuff.

II

In March 1980, with the automobile industry in the midst of one of the worst years in its history, officials of the Carter administration announced that the cost structure of U.S. producers was better than that of the Europeans and more or less on a par with that of the Japanese. They did so in the service of the politically convenient argument that the crisis in the industry was temporary and would pass as soon as domestic firms brought to market new and fuel-efficient models.

Speaking before the Subcommittee on Trade of the House Ways and Means Committee, Abraham Katz, then Assistant Secretary of Commerce for International Economic Policy, summarized the administration's view:

Average hourly compensation (including fringe benefits) in the Japanese auto industry in 1979 was $6.85—half of the $13.72 hourly compensation in the U.S. auto industry. Present indications are that productivity in the U.S. and Japanese auto industries may be roughly equal. On this basis Japanese producers appear to have had an $860 labor cost advantage per car in 1979. Other differential costs (principally the higher cost of steel in the United States) may have added $100 per car to the U.S. cost. As freight and insurance on Japanese cars average $400, the apparent cost advantage to Japanese producers may have been considerably less, for the above calculations do not take into account energy costs, capital costs, and the costs of other production factors—some of which are cheaper in the United States than in Japan.[2]

This view of things had many advocates outside the government. In 1978, for example, Ford published a study that placed the Japanese cost advantage per car at $500 and ascribed it to lower wage rates.[3] Reports by various academic and industry experts pegged the cost differential at an even lower figure than Ford's.[4] In none of this discussion, moreover, was there the slightest hint that Japanese manufacturers might be more productive than American. After all, the U.S. industry had long been renowned for its high level of mechanization, the sophistication of its materials and production-control systems, and its expertise in high-volume/low-cost operations. And—as chapter 3 makes clear—this reputation had been fairly earned. The classic Model T had taken 73 labor hours to assemble and its four-cylinder engine 23 hours to build; the 1972 Ford Mustang, by contrast, took only 27 labor hours to assemble and its four-cylinder engine a scant 6.2 hours to build.[5] Adjustment of these figures to reflect differences in product complexity over time would further increase, not decrease, the size of the reduction in labor requirements.

Progress of this sort was not limited to the major firms. Government data on the level of output per unit of labor input (the inverse of the labor content ratio) show a steady upward march of some 3 to 4 percent a year for the whole domestic industry, including parts suppliers.[6] True, there were some year-to-year fluctuations and, true, other countries have enjoyed more rapid rates of productivity growth, but their efforts started from a much lower base and so their improvements have been deceptively rapid. All in all, studies conducted up through the early 1970s showed the U.S. automobile industry to be the most productive in the world. In 1973, for example, the British Central Policy Staff estimated that the Americans were almost twice as productive (as measured by the number of vehicles per employee per year) as the French and Germans and three times as productive as the British.[7] The advantage over Japan was less—a 40 percent edge in labor efficiency—but it was substantial nonetheless.

Here, then, was cause for optimism. When the Carter administration judged the industry's difficulties in 1980 to be temporary, it was in effect taking the industry at its own earlier estimation. If domestic producers assumed an operational superiority over all competitors, the Carterites reasoned, not even an externally-imposed oil shock could long delay the introduction of efficient new products at more than competitive costs. Unfortunately, this confidence was badly misplaced.

In the first place, the true cost position of American firms was far more troublesome than the administration's optimistic view of things acknowledged. Table 5.1 presents a comparison of compensation levels for major U.S. and Japanese producers in 1981.[8] Since a typical small car represents a total of some eighty labor hours, by our calculations, the $8.72 per hour difference ($20 − $11.28) accounts—by itself—for a Japanese cost advantage of $700 per vehicle. But this is just the beginning. When we add into these calculations some correction for differences in costs among suppliers and for differences

TABLE 5.1

Annual Compensation of Production Workers and Employer
Cost per Hour Worked United States versus Japan

	United States	Japan
Standard Wage (base pay, cost-of-living adjustments, vacation pay)	$22,210	$10,349
Bonus	—	4,820
Allowances (housing, meals, commuting) and Overtime	1,306	3,517
Fringe Benefits	8,884	2,177
Total	$32,400	$20,863
Average Hours Worked Per Year	1,620	1,850
Total Cost Per Hour Worked	$20.00	$11.28

SOURCE: See appendix A.
NOTE: Not all of the listed compensation appears on a worker's paycheck. For example, fringe benefits include employer contributions to medical insurance. Average hours worked per year is the number of hours actually spent performing work. It *excludes* hours on rest breaks, vacations, and absences.

60

in labor productivity, the $700 figure proves way too low. Making these corrections, however, is a complicated business, for individual producers vary considerably in their mix of products and in their degree of vertical integration. (See appendix B for a discussion of our methodology.)

The process of analysis may be difficult, but the picture that emerges is disturbingly clear. As table 5.2 indicates, Japanese firms take many fewer labor hours to produce a small car than do their U.S. competitors, with the result that their true labor cost advantage lies somewhere between $1100 and $1400 per vehicle. Further, compared with American firms, the Japanese spend $600 to $800 less per vehicle on purchased materials and components. This figure reflects operations at suppliers, whose wage rate differentials are at least as great, but whose labor productivity differentials are smaller, than those of the major firms. Evidence developed by the U.S. Department of Transportation and our own discussions with industry analysts suggest that Japanese suppliers use only 20 to 25 percent fewer hours per vehicle than do their American counterparts.

Determined not to overstate the size of the Japanese advantage, we have checked these aggregate figures against the labor hours involved in the production of specific components. Table 5.3 summarizes our findings: a marked Japanese advantage in each of the operations studied, although the magnitude of the differences in labor hours does vary with the type of operation. We have

TABLE 5.2

Comparative Costs and Labor Productivity in Selected United States and Japanese Automobile Companies (1981)

Productivity/Cost Category	Ford	GM	Toyo Kogyo	Nissan
Labor Productivity				
Employee Hours per				
Small Car	84	83	53	51
Costs Per Small Car				
Labor	$1,848	$1,826	$ 620	$ 593
Purchased Components				
and Material	3,650	3,405	2,858	2,858
Other Manufacturing				
Costs	650	730	350	350
Nonmanufacturing				
Costs	350	325	1,100	1,200
Total	$6,498	$6,286	$4,928	$5,001

SOURCE: See appendix A.
NOTE: Nonmanufacturing costs include the costs of ocean freight (for the Japanese producers), selling, and administrative expenses. Other manufacturing costs include costs of warranty, capital costs, energy costs, and miscellaneous items like insurance.

not studied in detail every part of the manufacturing process; but where we have looked, the data confirm the general estimates presented in tables 5.2 and 5.3. This productivity gap is not, moreover, the result of clever manipulation of statistics, disparate reporting conventions, or incomplete accounting. (There are not enough Japanese workers hidden away on the rolls of captive suppliers or subcontractors to explain the consistently more productive operation of Japanese plants and factories.) The productivity gap is every bit as real, every bit as tangible, as differences in materials costs or rates of compensation.

By itself, however, Japan's edge in labor productivity is of uncertain meaning, for it might reflect nothing more than a wholesale substitution of machinery for people. To see if this is indeed the case, we have taken a look at the relative productivity of capital of both U.S. and Japanese producers. Once again, the analysis is complicated but its implications, painfully obvious. Table 5.4 compares on a per vehicle basis both the reported book (historical cost) value and the replacement value of the capital stock, expressed in dollars, for Ford, GM, Toyo Kogyo, and Nissan. We use 1979 data because 1979 was the most recent year during which the U.S. producers enjoyed levels of capacity utilization comparable to those of the Japanese. Even the most cursory glance at table 5.4 refutes the argument that Japan has achieved its edge in labor productivity by the simple substitution of capital for labor. The unpleasant truth is that Japanese producers use less capital to produce a vehicle than do their U.S. competitors and can sustain a given volume of production with much lower levels of investment. What makes this truth unpleasant is that the Japanese advantage rests not on a substitution of capital for labor or labor for capital; it rests, instead, on diligent control of the whole system of production.

Differences in capital costs per vehicle appear under "other manufacturing costs" in table 5.2. Not even the higher expenses Japanese producers incur for ocean freight, duties, marketing, and distribution (summarized as "non-manufacturing costs" in table 5.2) can offset their substantial advantage in all

TABLE 5.3

U.S.–Japanese Differences in Labor Hours per Small Car in Selected Plants (1980)

	United States	Japan
Assembly	28	17
Engine	7	4
Stamping	10	4
Transmission	8	6

SOURCE: See appendix A.
NOTE: All operations corrected for differences in vertical integration.

TABLE 5.4

*Productivity of Capital in Automobile Production in Selected
U.S. and Japanese Companies (1979)*

	Ford	GM	Toyo Kogyo	Nissan
Capital Per Vehicle				
Reported book value				
(historical cost)	$3,048	$2,123	$1,351	$1,484
Replacement value	$5,052	$4,394	$2,161	$2,344

SOURCE: See appendix A.
NOTE: Capital is defined as the value of plant, equipment, and inventories.
Reported book value is the value of the plant, equipment, and inventories as
originally purchased. Replacement value is what the plant, equipment, and
inventory would cost if it had to be replaced today.

of the other measurements of performance here employed (compensation
rates, labor productivity, capital costs). A small Japanese car, packed into a
freighter and shipped across the Pacific, lands on an American dock with a
cost advantage over comparable U.S. products of something between $1200
and $1500, conservatively estimated.

Harry Truman, it is said, often wished for the advice of a one-handed economist because his regular economic advisors always qualified their recommen-
dations by saying "But, on the other hand . . ." To this extent, though to no
other, Truman would appreciate these findings. With reference to the landed
cost advantage of Japanese cars, there is no "other hand." Fifteen hundred
dollars is the inescapable truth.

III

As we noted earlier, Japanese producers have not been content idly to skim
off the profits implied by their landed cost advantage. They have, instead, lev-
eraged that advantage by following closely—after an initial false start—the
early lesson of VW in the American market: success in building market share
goes to those entrants that combine low price with perceived high performance
and quality. Much more than either performance or price, however, quality
is an attribute that is extremely difficult to define in practice. American consumers, immune to these conceptual problems, have given a rather clear indication of where they stand on the matter. In a 1981 survey conducted by
the American Society for Quality Control, several American products—

pharmaceuticals, for example, and frozen foods—had ratings of 50 percent or better as being of high or very high quality. By contrast, only 17.6 percent of the respondents viewed U.S.-built automobiles as being of high or very high quality.[9]

These findings are instructive, but only as a starting point. To make usable sense out of them, we must understand both what lies behind consumer perceptions of inadequate quality and where—in the design, engineering, and production processes—even well-intentioned efforts might go astray. We may begin by observing that, because automobiles are multidimensional products built up out of many complex subsystems, consumer perceptions of quality tend to cluster about several different kinds of attributes: styling, luxury, performance, workmanship (fits and finishes), reliability, and durability. In searching for measures of quality that are comparable across models and market segments, we have decided to focus on the last three of these attributes: workmanship, reliability, and durability.

This requires a word of explanation. Many domestic consumers regard a car with luxurious interior, stately dimensions, and "boulevard" ride as being of high quality; others attach that label to a car with functional interior, aerodynamic styling, quick acceleration, and responsive handling. How to choose between them? In point of fact, there is no reasonable way to do so, for these cars were designed for quite different purposes and were intended to satisfy quite different sets of preferences. Evaluations of quality based on workmanship, reliability, and durability, however, would apply to both cars. It requires no leap of faith to believe that most consumers would view a car with obvious streaks in the paint job, windows that do not roll all the way up, doors that do not hang right, an engine that leaks oil, and an electrical system that fails after 500 miles as being of lower quality than a competitor's product without these failings. So much is common sense.

Table 5.5 summarizes available data on the first of these attributes, workmanship. The quality of an automobile's fits and finishes—what the industry calls "showroom quality"—is a function of its exterior fittings, trim, moldings, alignment of doors, hood, and trunk, paint job, interior appointments, and dashboard assembly. Quality here is largely determined by attention to detail in the final assembly plant, but responsibility also extends back to design and engineering activities. If, for example, tolerances and alignments for passenger-side doors established by the design process are in error or if stamping plants fail to meet their sheet metal specifications, quality is as directly affected as it would be by shoddy assembly work. Nor need there be out-and-out errors in design to throw final quality off. Cars can be designed in a way that frustrates close attention to detail.

The first column of table 5.5 gives representative consumer ratings, based

TABLE 5.5

Evidence on Workmanship: A Comparison of U.S. and Japanese Automobiles (1979)

Country/Model	Consumer Ratings[1] (condition of car at delivery)	Defects per Vehicle Shipped (after one month)
United States		
Chevrolet Chevette	7.2	3.00
Ford Pinto	6.5	3.70
VW Rabbit	7.8	2.13
Dodge Omni	7.4	4.10
Plymouth Horizon	7.5	NA
Japan		
Toyota Corolla	7.8	0.71[2]
Honda Civic	8.0	1.23[3]
Mitsubishi Colt	7.8	NA

SOURCES: Rogers National Research, *Buyer Profiles,* 1979; discussions with industry executives.
NOTES: 1. Scale of 1 to 10; 10 = excellent.
      2. Toyota average.
      3. Honda average.

on a 1979 nationwide survey of new car buyers, for overall vehicle condition at delivery. The slight edge here given to Japanese products is considerably increased by the data in the second column. After owning their new cars for one month, U.S. consumers reported an average of three to five times more defects (a defect being anything that does not work and needs to be fixed—faulty wipers, loose bolts, and all) in the domestically-built products. Remember, too, that these one-month figures come *after* factory inspection and *after* dealer preparation. Moreover, evidence on warranty costs suggests that neither the significance of the problems with Japanese cars nor the magnitude of repair costs are enough to offset the advantage they enjoy from a low incidence of defects.[10]

Simply stated, these findings suggest that Japanese cars are, at least initially, put together better. But do they stay that way? Repair incidence data published by Consumer's Union on the basis of information supplied by subscribers to *Consumer Reports* give a mixed verdict. As reported in table 5.6, Japanese cars are rated substantially higher on reliability of the body (problems with paint, corrosion, windows, doors, seats, water leaks, noise, rattles, squeaks, and the like), with most all of the difference coming in body integrity and hardware and virtually none in resistance to corrosion. In terms of mechanical reliability, Japanese and American products are rated much closer (the former come out ahead on fuel-delivery systems, electrical systems, and automatic transmissions; the latter, on brakes; both are even on engines, drive-train, exhaust, ignition, suspension, and manual transmissions).

This evidence is broadly consistent with that cited earlier on consumer perceptions. Body and trim, where the Japanese excel in both workmanship and reliability, have a disproportionately great influence on what consumers view as quality in automobiles. With systems less immediately visible to the consumer or with aspects of quality that only become apparent after a lapse of years, the Japanese advantage decreases or disappears altogether. The advantage exists, but it is by no means insurmountable. Such, at least, is the implication of table 5.7, which displays *Consumer Reports* data on the operating problems of cars five to six years old.

Whatever the niceties here, the plain fact remains that consumer perceptions about quality do influence sales, and the landed-cost advantage enjoyed by Japanese producers translates those sales into a highly profitable stream of revenues. This is the basis on which Japanese manufacturers of automobiles—and, for that matter, of a host of other products—have been able to compete so very successfully with domestic American producers. These, in short, are the inescapable terms of the new industrial competition.

But to say this, of course, is not enough, for it implicitly raises but does not answer the central question: where does the Japanese advantage come from? Market-appealing quality, relatively low wage rates, and relatively high labor productivity are all well and good, but they mean little unless they can

TABLE 5.6

Ratings of Reliability of U.S. and Japanese Cars (1981)

Country/Model	Body	Mechanical
United States		
Chevrolet Chevette	8.8	9.6
VW Rabbit	10.0	10.0
Dodge Omni	7.5	9.6
Ford Escort	10.0	9.6
Japan		
Toyota Corolla	13.8	12.3
Honda Civic	15.0	11.9
Mitsubishi Colt	13.8	11.2
Datsun 210	15.0	10.8
Mazda GLC	13.8	9.6

SOURCE: *Consumer Reports* (April, 1982).
NOTE: The numbers in the table are average ratings of frequency of repair, as made by readers of *Consumer Reports*. The numbers are based on a scoring system, ranging from 0 to 20 as follows: 0=Far Below Average, 10=Average, 20=Far Above Average.

TABLE 5.7

Evidence on Durability of U.S. and Japanese Cars (1981)

Country/Model (1976 models)	Corrosion	Body Average	Engine Mechanical	Electro-Mechanical Average
United States				
Chevrolet Chevette	20	16.3	10	9.2
Ford Pinto	5	6.3	0	8.8
Chevrolet Nova	10	8.8	15	7.7
Ford Maverick	10	10.0	10	8.8
Buick Century	10	15.0	20	12.5
Dodge Dart	10	7.5	15	7.7
Japan				
Toyota Corolla	20	20.0	10	16.9
Mitsubishi Colt	15	12.5	10	13.5
Honda Civic	5	8.3	10	10.4
Datsun 210	0	7.5	10	13.5
Toyota Corona	15	18.8	15	17.0
Honda Accord	0	12.5	0	13.5
Datsun 710	5	7.5	10	10.4

SOURCE: *Consumer Reports* (April, 1982).
NOTE: The numbers in the table are average ratings of frequency of repair for five-year-old cars, as made by readers of *Consumer Reports*. The numbers are based on a scoring system, ranging from 0 to 20 as follows: 0=Far Below Average, 10= Average, 20=Far Above Average. These data are *not* based on a comparison of cars operated under identical conditions or identical programs of maintenance.

be carefully deployed as strategic assets. Each by itself can, as Shakespeare has Cassius say of Mark Antony, "do no more than Caesar's arm/ When Caesar's head is off." To be of value they must be managed, be part of a coherent whole, have a clear-cut purpose to serve. The differences between Japanese and American automakers in productivity, cost, and quality are important less in themselves than as reflections of an achieved excellence in manufacturing. They are not causes, but results; not motive agents, but symptoms. It is the hard-won ability to devise and maintain a world-class manufacturing system that comes first.

Chapter 6

A Paradigm for Production

NESTLED among the rolling hills of Saugus, Massachusetts, is an old iron mill built by Scottish artisans in the seventeenth century. The mill is a state park now, its fiery hearth quietly restored but the whole long since transformed into a place of grass and flowers and strolling tourists. If one takes a deliberate step back from these bucolic sights and visually strips away the intervening centuries, one can almost see the hardy Scots at their work turning ore into iron. More to the point, one can also see that the way they did their work—for all its brute simplicity when compared with the integrated steel mills of today—contains in embryo almost every ingredient essential to the modern production process. It is true, of course, that any twentieth-century facility of U.S. Steel or Inland or Armco would dwarf both in size and complexity the activities at Saugus, but it is equally true that the structure of an Armco or Inland or U.S. Steel mill was already present in those seventeenth-century operations.

Recognizing this historical continuity is important because it suggests that the evolution of production systems does not occur in a haphazard fashion. Advances in process technology tend to take place within a certain fundamental structure of operations that, in terms of an industry's development over time, crystallizes quite early on. No matter how far-reaching the changes in its technology, an industry's underlying paradigm of production often gets established relatively early and then changes relatively little. Although obvious surface differences in process cry out for attention, the careful observer will pause to note underlying structural likenesses. In the world of manufacturing as in the world of nature, there is not an infinite variety of radically different ways to achieve the same ends—be those ends the production of an ingot of steel or the construction of a ball-and-socket joint. There is, by contrast, a rather limited range of basic possibilities, each of which allows immense latitude for evolutionary modification and adaptation.

For steel, the selection among these possibilities was already implicit in the Saugus works; for automobiles, a much younger industry than steel, it was contained in the production system that Henry Ford put together in the early years of this century to mass produce a low-cost vehicle. Then as now, the operations of every major producer took as their starting point similar equipment, processes, and techniques. This similarity has persisted through time (and can be seen today in factories in Tokyo, Paris, Detroit, and elsewhere) not because all firms insist on copying from each other but because all understand equally well the necessary operational structure for manufacturing automobiles.

No wonder, then, it has proven difficult to admit or explain the substantial Japanese advantages in productivity, cost, and quality outlined in the previous chapter. If all firms in the industry go about the work of manufacturing in pretty much the same way, how is it that the Japanese have done such a better job of it? This, of course, has been a common refrain in recent years and has given rise to any number of specious arguments. Perhaps the most familiar of them is the notion that Japan's success stems from the prodigal use of plants and machines that are newer and thus more efficient than those available in America. Unfortunately for adherents of this "new plant" argument, the Japanese actually use less capital per vehicle than do their American counterparts (see appendix B). Nor, for that matter, do they use more advanced process technologies.

The relevant differences lie elsewhere. The exemplary productivity, cost, and quality record of Japanese automobile makers is explicable not in terms of "new plant" or "new technology" but, instead, in the way automobile production is managed. The Japanese have accepted and expanded Ford's insight into the fundamental structure of fifth-stage production and have devoted considerable energies to mastering the manufacturing agenda it implies.

II

For industrial journalists before World War I, as for the general public, Ford's manufacturing accomplishments were an unending source of wonder and amazement.[1] No man or institution had ever tried to build so complex a product in so large a volume or to bring together so many precise mechanical operations on so regular a basis. Nonetheless, the major "firsts" often ascribed to Ford—the concepts of mass production and the moving assembly line—were not firsts at all. Mass production had, at least in general terms, previously been put to work in a host of other industries; the boat builders of fifteenth-century Venice had perfected the idea of a moving assembly line. Ford's real contribution lay in his understanding of the necessary structure of automobile manufacturing and, by extension, of the agenda of essential tasks. More particularly, he saw that the sheer magnitude of the undertaking (providing on demand to many thousands of workers thousands of complex parts made to exacting specifications) created unprecedented challenges to production planning and control.[2]

Managing quality, equipment, inventory, and people on such a scale was an entirely new kind of problem, but a problem that would have to be solved if the mass production of automobiles were to become a reality. Finding solutions to these bewildering difficulties in planning and control was, thus, the agenda Ford set for himself. And his practical response to that agenda was to structure his activities according to two basic concepts: specialization and progressive production.[3]

Specialization as applied by Ford affected everything: machines were to be designed to do only one thing; plants were to be dedicated to the production of only one kind of part; workers, whether in the office or on the factory floor, were to be assigned only a few limited tasks. By standardizing work in this fashion, Ford hoped to make the responsibilities of men, equipment, and systems simpler, easier to discharge, and easier to control. As the jobs once performed exclusively by skilled machinists or engineers or mechanics were broken up and distributed among less skilled workers who had been taught the use of specialized machines, the resulting mechanization of production allowed large numbers of not particularly well-trained workers to turn out a product every bit as good as that built in earlier years by highly expert craftsmen. More to the point, it allowed them to turn out such products at a much lower cost and in much larger volume.

This emphasis on specialization made possible, in turn, Ford's reliance on progressive production. Rather than deposit a full complement of parts in one place and put a car together from the ground up, Ford organized his operations into a carefully defined sequence of stages. Parts were themselves constructed on a step-by-step basis and were then brought together on a rigorous schedule at the sub-assembly or assembly level. For all the attention it has received, the moving assembly line was only one—albeit the most representative—element of this whole deliberately orchestrated process. True, it epitomized better than anything else the "progressive" concept on which the process rested, but it worked as well as it did not because of some special excellence of its own but because it was so fully integrated into a coherent production system.

With operations organized sequentially, inventory requirements declined, although they did not completely disappear. Machines broke down from time to time, and having a buffer of inventory ready at hand meant that other activities could proceed while repairs were made. Yet it was a mistake to permit that buffer to grow too large. Finding the right balance among the length of production runs, the cost of setting up machines for those runs, and the cost of carrying inventory allowed managers to amortize expenses over the greatest number of parts (which lowered average costs) while protecting against interruptions in production (which raised them).

As a mode of organization, then, progressive production created a series of work centers separated from each other by in-process inventory and by the conveyors and transfer devices used to move that inventory along. There arose, quite naturally, an enhanced need to coordinate all pieces of the system, for linking things together in so interdependent a fashion placed a premium on management's ability to synchronize them appropriately. This, of course, meant even better control over the timely flow of information, a task increasingly entrusted to a new kind of specialist: the production clerk.[4] No ordinary, green eye-shaded keeper of the books, the production clerk had to be an expert in tracking parts, spotting bottlenecks, shortages, or slowdowns, and expediting their removal. Over time these functions became institutionalized in production control departments with their own internal rules and procedures, just as other specialized functions—the oversight of quality or personnel or the purchase of materials—gradually took on their own institutional forms.

If Ford's manufacturing agenda implied new kinds of specialized expertise, it also implied—as we pointed out in chapter 3—a certain specialization of suppliers, who concentrated on a single component, as well as unskilled blue-collar workers, who concentrated on a specific task. As Ford himself understood, "The net result of the application of these principles is the reduction of the necessity of thought on the part of the worker and the reduction of his movements to a minimum. He does as nearly as possible only one thing with only one movement."[5] In this scheme of things, workers were doers, not thinkers. Their only task was to keep up with the rhythmic flow of production at a pace set by machines.

To monitor these efforts required yet another kind of expert: a specialist in keeping the pressure on. Not surprisingly, these new monitors or supervisors bore little relation to the jack-of-all-trades foremen of the nineteenth century, for their job was to see that nothing held up the closely timed flow of production.[6] The adversarial relationship between workers and supervisors grew worse as workers increasingly came to be viewed as doers, not thinkers. Nor did it improve with the unionization of the labor force during the 1930s and 1940s. If anything, the arrival of written contracts and collective bargaining—although they gave workers a larger voice in setting conditions of work—made the adversarial nature of shop floor relations even more explicit.

The paradigm for large-scale manufacturing to which Ford's principles of specialization and progressive production gave birth found a ready home in other industries confronted by the dual requirements of high volume and low cost. There, as in the automobile industry, manufacturing became an increasingly integrated and mechanized activity—an activity in which inventory was used as a buffer against the failure of equipment, people, or materials and in which staff specialists monitored, inspected, audited, scheduled, planned, and supervised the limited tasks of individual workers. Managing the immense human effort to produce at high volume demanded precisely this kind of operational structure; and, as we have argued in chapter 2, the inexorable logic of production economies demanded high volume.

Indeed, "getting metal out the door" rapidly became the automobile industry's basic measure of success at the plant level, for the marketplace merely served to reinforce the technology- and cost-driven pressures toward a standardized, flow-type system of production. Managers had to worry, of course, about their ability to meet changing consumer preferences for different models and options, but fine-tuning the product mix inevitably took a back seat to their primary job: during good times, getting as much metal as possible out the door, seven days a week, three shifts a day; during bad times, laying off workers and cutting back on capacity until demand strengthened again. Even as late as the mid-1970s, these were still the prime managerial tools for adjusting to cyclical fluctuations in demand.

III

To see how the Japanese manage the production of automobiles, we undertook an extensive tour of their factories.[7] We began with the bustling multi-plant complex of Toyo Kogyo, the Hiroshima-based maker of Mazda cars and trucks. It was a good place to begin, for Toyo Kogyo, long a technical leader in the Japanese industry (it was the first company to employ robots, the first to apply computer-controlled assembly, and the first to mass produce the rotary engine), had come close to bankruptcy during the mid-1970s.

Perched on the brink of disaster, management introduced a stringent cost control program and launched a full-scale effort to rationalize production. In other words, Toyo Kogyo had just been fighting for its life on the basis of excellence in manufacturing.

The battle had gone well. Productivity rose dramatically; work-in-process inventory fell from a seven-day level in April, 1975, to a two to three-day level in 1981; and the number of labor hours per vehicle plummeted from 96.9 in 1974 to 66 in 1977—a 30 percent reduction in a two-year period.[8] What was responsible for these striking improvements? Our interviews with Toyo Kogyo managers came back time and again to the commitment of employees, the personal style of managers, and the underlying concepts of production. As a project manager in the production planning group explained these concepts to us, they had a familiar ring: "to provide what is needed by the customer at a reasonable price at the highest level of quality within the shortest possible period of time."

Here, again, was the same structural problem that had confronted Henry Ford the better part of a century ago. And here, too, was an effort to solve that problem in a manner of which Ford would have heartily approved: make the production system correspond at all levels (even down to the individual metalworking operation) as closely as possible to the flow of water through a pipeline. In practice, of course, this meant synchronizing activities so as to eliminate bottlenecks and inventory floats wherever possible, an up-to-date application of Ford's notion of progressive production. In Toyo Kogyo's hands, it meant reliance on a "just-in-time" inventory system that transferred parts from one operation to the next precisely when they were needed and in the precise quantity needed.[9]

But if Ford would have approved this "progressive" system, he would have been troubled by its logic. It has long been axiomatic that setting up machines for production runs is expensive, that long production runs allow those costs to be amortized over a large number of items, and that keeping an inventory buffer ready at hand—though also expensive—offsets the even greater expense of numerous machine setups.[10] For years the trade-off between the costs of a reasonable level of inventory and the costs of short production runs favored the stockpiling of inventory. Toyo Kogyo's reliance on the just-in-time system, however, allowed virtually no stockpiling and required short production runs, frequent setups, and the organization of machinery not by type but by sequence of operations.

This sense of being in the presence of something familiar yet oddly different stayed with us throughout our time in Japanese factories. The manufacturing agenda to which these facilities were devoted gave us no pause. Nor did the equipment in use—the tunnel broaches, boring machines, transfer lines, welding guns, sheet metal presses, and assembly lines (which drew parts past each worker at about the speed first set by Henry Ford in 1914). When, however, an assembly line shut down, its alarms flashing, our feeling of "sameness" began to evaporate.

In an American plant, the foremen and machine operators would try to puzzle out what had gone wrong, would call in the appropriate craftsmen to fix it, and would dicker at length about which skilled trades had jurisdiction over which parts of the problem. Employment contracts and both management and union policies restrict the kinds of things (maintenance, repair) that an operator is allowed to do. At Toyo Kogyo, by contrast, the operator immediately began to work on his own machine with the help of the foreman while nearby workers pitched in to clear the line of clogged work-in-process. In 1981, teamwork of this sort kept downtime for Toyo Kogyo's transfer lines to but 3.9 percent—and for car body welding lines to but 1.4 percent—of operational time.[11] The comparable numbers for American plants are much higher.

We consider these issues of work force attitude and management at length in chapter 7; here we are more interested in exploring how the basic principles on which Japanese manufacturers have organized their efforts represent a distinctive and consistent response to the same problems faced by American producers. Thus, with the novel logic of Toyo Kogyo's inventory policy fresh in our minds, we next studied certain automated processes at Mitsubishi's Okazaki assembly and stamping plant.

Surrounded by rice fields tilled in the ancient manner, the Okazaki complex was interesting to us for its reliance on a computer-activated process for welding auto bodies. In America, only a few plants—Ford's Ohio truck plant (new in 1975) among them—have attempted to match the on-line automation at the Okazaki facility in the variety of models that can be run down the same body assembly line. This mixed-model approach, which is dependent only in part on automated processes, allows cars without a great measure of commonality of parts to be put together in a specified sequence on the same line. And this, in turn, allows companies to offer a richer product mix at lower volumes without inefficient levels of investment. The agenda-based goal is still progressive production, but the means to achieve it do not necessarily include the long production runs of fully standardized items that are the American norm.

Not all Japanese producers, of course, follow this mixed-model system religiously. Some, like Honda, apply it to certain of their assembly plants but not to others. Even where they do apply it, they do not always apply it in identical fashion. A mistake well worth avoiding, therefore, is trying to view all mixed-model efforts as constituting a discrete organizational approach, which is fixed in technique and unalterably opposed to a single-model orientation. The truth is more complicated than that. To be sure, these efforts represent a different kind of production orientation, but only in the most general terms. How it gets applied in specific manufacturing contexts has as much to do with the distinctive philosophy of individual Japanese companies as with the possibilities inherent in the technology.

Each Japanese producer searches in its own way to find a competitive edge in its manufacturing process and has its own distinctive preference about how things should be done. Consider, for example, how Mitsubishi and Nissan address themselves to the task of mounting doors, a task of some importance to a buyer's valuation of a car's overall quality of "fit and finish." At the Okazaki plant, as a car body moves into position, a worker removes a door from a rack and bolts it onto the frame at the hinges. The worker then opens and shuts the door to test its swing before stepping back to inspect its alignment visually. If things are not quite right, the worker will take out a rubber-headed mallet and whack the door a few times until it fits properly. The whole process takes less than a minute.

At Nissan's Zama plant, however, doors are mounted twice. They are first bolted to the frame for painting in order to get the color match right, then removed and trimmed separately from the body before being mounted again at the end of the assembly process. A sophisticated mounting device holds the door in position while a worker bolts it on. No rubber mallets are needed or used.

Placing a high value on simplicity and low capital investment, Mitsubishi has hit upon a different procedure than has Nissan, which prefers to assemble the inside of the car before finally mounting doors. To cite another example, Honda emphasizes high quality operations at high line speeds (some sixty-five cars per hour on a given assembly line); Nissan is more comfortable with slower line speeds (thirty cars per hour), shorter—if more capital-intensive—assembly lines, and more varied work assignments.

Do not, however, be misled by these variations in corporate personality; they are but variations on a single common theme: ironclad adherence to the strict discipline of a just-in-time inventory system. There are, it turns out, many different ways to put that discipline into practice, but the commitment to doing so dwarfs in importance all idiosyncratic modes of application. In fact, this just-in-time production system lies at the heart of the Japanese manufacturing paradigm. It is quite different from the American "just-in-case" view, which treats inventory as a hedge against the interruption of the long production runs of standardized items mandated by the gospel of scale economies. For the Japanese, however, prudence is not a function of smoothing over possible difficulties but, rather, of stripping away all covers so that the source of problems can be identified and removed. To their way of thinking, inventory is a place in which problems can lie hidden. Strip away the camouflage, pull the chain as tight as possible, and the weakest links—the hidden flaws in the production system—will become obvious.

This determination to make all problems visible is not an unmixed blessing.[12] It offers the hope of thoroughly efficient operations by substantially raising the social costs and consequences of failure. Reducing inventory levels places increasing pressure on managers and workers alike to solve whatever problems remain—that is, it directs energy and initiative where they belong by ratcheting up the level of stress at which the work force is expected to perform. In Japan, making problems organizationally visible means making them socially visible as well and, thus, quickly bringing to bear the efforts of coworkers and foremen to resolve them. As rough-hewn characters have long been wont to observe, it is wonderful how a little bit of fear and danger can clear the mind.

Fear and danger, however, can just as easily cloud performance—unless, that is, workers are carefully integrated into a system designed to support their efforts. Consequently, production equipment in Japan often has foolproof mechanical safeguards against innocently passing along defective parts to the next operation. Workers also make numerous visual inspections of work-in-process, and indicator boards at each station flash yellow lights to indicate problems or red lights to indicate work stoppages.

Visual control, much more than the state-of-the-art computerized systems employed by American factories, also determines inventory levels.[13] This system, called "Kanban" after the little cards or tickets it uses, operates much like a supermarket and its warehouse.[14] Just as a warehouse manager will forward only those products ordered by the store manager (and only in the quantity ordered), so the Kanban system requires work centers to make and send parts to each other only as they receive Kanban cards telling them to do so. The rule of thumb for upstream units is, quite simply, make nothing until you get a Kanban and then only in the standard amount; for downstream units, the rule is, do not order parts until you need them and then order only the standard amount. As long as all participants follow these rules and allow user needs to pull parts through the system, the number of Kanban outstanding determines the level of inventory. The objective, of course, is to have as few Kanban in circulation as possible.

In the management of inventory, as of all production-related activities, the Japanese showed themselves to be doggedly persistent in their efforts to master operational detail.[15] We had been half-prepared to find them using process technology far more advanced than anything available to their American counterparts. What we saw about us at every turn, however, was not newer technology but better management of the technology in place—not the exotic gimmickry of wide-eyed public expectation but a sober mastery of manufacturing.

A Paradigm for Production

At Toyota's fifteen-year-old Kamigo engine plant, for example, the modern tooling we had recently seen in Detroit's most advanced engine plant was not there. Instead, what we found was that the Kamigo operation used about half as many labor hours to produce an engine as did the Detroit plant with its elegant systems for the laser inspection of machined parts, its complex control systems for machine tools, and its cutting-edge processing equipment. Nor was this some trick of light-fingered bookkeeping. Both facilities produced roughly the same number of parts in-house; neither relied on extensive vendor-supplied labor. The productivity difference was real.

Again, at Nissan's Zama facility, where articles in the business press had readied us to see how "Robots Do the Work on Datsuns," we discovered robots at work in the body shop and in the welding operation, but that was all.[16] In fact, we observed a rather large (100 car) buffer inventory for the painting operation, which was scheduled separately from and was therefore not synchronized with final assembly. When that inventory queue filled up, the assembly line—with all its robots and automated equipment—shut down while workers performed maintenance chores. To our expressions of surprise, Nissan managers replied that they were far more concerned with the quality of painting and welding than with the efficient use of capital. Like the managers at Toyota in spirit but unlike them in the choices made, they had a very clear idea of where in their manufacturing process they could find a company-specific key to competitive advantage.

IV

It is a truism, of course, that not every Japanese manufacturer chooses to compete in precisely the same way, but it is equally true that Japanese participants in large-volume, capital-intensive industries do tend to rely on their mastery of labor productivity, product quality, rapid new product development, and the ability of their manufacturing systems to accommodate product diversity. Simple-minded efforts to link these shared competencies to the age of capital stock, the discipline of workers, the cultural response to authority, or the individual's attention to detail miss the point. There is no secret formula for Japan's recent industrial success, no miraculous absence of labor strife or job hopping or interpersonal difficulties. There is, instead, only an insistent effort to manage the whole manufacturing process as a coherent, integrated system. American companies that have felt the weight of Japanese competition might wish otherwise, but this particular mystery of the East is no mystery at all.

77

On the basis of our research and of what we saw in Japan, we would con-
clude that, on balance, Japanese manufacturing systems keep their lines operational a higher percentage of the time, make greater use of materials-handling
equipment, process fewer defective parts, enjoy lower rates of worker absenteeism, and match workers better with their tasks then do most comparable systems in the United States. These strengths are related, for they are all the direct
result of a production philosophy that stresses not volume, as does the American philosophy, but quality—of process as well as product. By quality we mean
simply an emphasis on doing things right the first time—no defects, no mis-
takes, no misuse of machines, no activity that does not add value. If American
producers have been transfixed with the notion of getting metal out the door,
the Japanese have kept their eye on eliminating waste.

Faced with the same challenge of building automobiles, Japanese and American companies have responded differently. The latter, often beset with fluctuations in demand, chose to build a system dominated by scale economies
and long production runs and thus, by extension, the loss of flexibility inherent in standardization. The former, operating in an environment of rapid and
steady growth, built a system dominated by quality and the drive to eliminate waste, and they supported it by every means at their disposal. They established rigorously consistent practices for the management of equipment,
materials, and people; they achieved high machine utilization through almost
religious adherence to maintenance schedules and stable operating patterns;
they used a policy of just-in-time production to keep inventories low; and
they incorporated the work force as a fully integrated part of the whole production system.

In most American companies, management science determines how the various factors of production are to be bought and sold so as to optimize performance. Labor, like capital or materials or components, is a commodity—nothing more and nothing less. It is the stuff out of which efficient
transactions are concocted, and transactions drive the assembly lines. In
Japan, the work force is viewed as an integrated part of the manufacturing
system, as something to be carefully nurtured—a point we develop at greater
length in the next chapter. We overstate a little, to be sure. American practice
is not so uniformly bleak, nor have the more enlightened companies failed to
mend their ways. Nor, for that matter, are the Japanese uniformly successful.
But the differences between operations in the two countries are real, not the
fabrication of some human resources consultant. Americans buy and sell labor;
the Japanese build a production process around it.

We came away from our tour through Japanese factories more convinced
than ever that the status symbols of management often get in the way of
first-class operations, that narrowly defined jobs waste valuable human talent,

and that adversarial relationships between workers and managers need not be an inescapable fact of life. We did not—and do not—believe that Japanese workers are (or that American workers could be) filled with unbounded on-the-job happiness. Again, what the Japanese have deliberately done is treat their work force as a key point of competitive leverage. This has its costs—workers face the same grueling pressures that managers do—but extraordinary benefits as well. As one senior manager said to us, "As an individual you may be smarter than I am. But once I begin to work within my organization with my fellow workers, I am unbeatable."

All this, in a way, we had been prepared to see. We had read and heard enough about the Japanese paradigm for production that our on-the-spot explorations tended to confirm our expectations. Surprise came from a different quarter. That the Japanese had found their own distinctive way to face the same manufacturing agenda and to use the same hardware as American companies was axiomatic. That their approach shared a great deal with the early organization of American efforts was something else again. As Taichi Ohno, the architect of Toyota's production system, once remarked: "If Henry Ford were alive today, I am positive he would have done what we did with our Toyota production system."[17] For this notion we were not prepared.

Yet it makes sense. Implicit in Ford's activities in the early part of the century was a vision of how a production system should run—a vision that his own labors only partly achieved, a vision from which his own later efforts and those of other American producers increasingly diverged. Ohno's comment, combined with the lessons we drew from our inspection of modern-day Japanese factories, suggests a discomforting thought: American manufacturers have long shared in a rich patrimony that needed only diligent care and attention to confer great benefits. But for reasons that might at the time have seemed excellent, they turned away from that inheritance. Now they come back home in search of their roots. Like prodigal sons, they have put their heritage and inheritance at risk; unlike them, however, they find the keepers of the home fires to be not family, but strangers from the other side of the world.

A discomforting thought, surely, but one that is also full of hope, for it argues that what is of lasting value in the way the Japanese manage inventory, quality, productivity, and people is not bounded by an alien culture but is instead part of our own. Henry Ford's vigorous emphasis on the design and fabrication of advanced machine tools, his relentless drive to rationalize production and reduce in-process inventory, his push to make all process flows continuous, his reliance on materials-handling equipment, and his focus on simple designs and precision machining—all these and more are part of current Japanese practice. Nor was Ford convinced that he had solved the problems of production once and for all. Like the Japanese, he looked on the factory as a laboratory for which there was no grand, final design but which would always profit from experience to become ever more efficient.

Despite extensive backward integration into the production of iron, steel, rubber, wood, and fabric, Ford drove total inventories down from a level of 204 days in 1903 to 17 days in 1922, the heyday of the Model T. The impressive rationalization of current operations at Toyota and Nissan simply pales in comparison to what was achieved at Ford's Rouge River complex. Within forty-eight hours a load of iron ore delivered to the Rouge River docks was processed through the blast furnace, run through casting and finishing machines, and taken through final assembly. From iron ore to finished Model T in two days—here was process rationalization with a vengeance![18]

And here, as well, were the innovative volume-driven approaches to work force management essential to the smooth integration of human workers into the production system. As Anne Jardin writes of the early Ford organization:

A man could make his own job, assume responsibility where he felt fit. The job and how well it was done formed the basis of the relationship between Ford and his executives, none of whom . . . [was] boss in any formal sense. To help suppliers cut costs, Ford sent engineers into their plants to improve manufacturing methods [and] paid in advance for their products to give them capital for high volume machine tools.[19]

On the shop floor, as even Ford's bitterest critics acknowledged, a real comraderie existed, even if the need to foster it was not clear at the outset. By 1913, however, managers had begun to see that the human element in production required substantial attention.

John R. Lee, Ford's first personnel manager, remembered that transition in viewpoint:

We began to realize something of the relative value of men, machines and material, so to speak, and we confess that up to this time we believed that mechanism and material were of larger importance and that somehow or other the human element of our men was taken care of automatically and needed little or no consideration.[20]

What prompted the change was the variety of problems that surfaced in 1912–1913 and turned the factory gate into a revolving door. Workers came and went in droves. Turnover rates reached 60 percent per month, absenteeism soared, and the workers who did show up began to restrict output. If the ideal of progressive production were to be achieved, something would have to give.

What gave or, rather, what appeared was the justly famous "Five Dollar Day," an innovative form of profit sharing. Workers received their previous wage as base pay and were allowed to "participate in the profits" up to a level of five dollars per day if they met certain standards of sobriety, thriftiness, and hard work.[21] Other policies created additional incentives for workers to emulate certain models of industrious behavior. A Sociological Department was formed to shape the attitudes and habits of employees and to instill in them a set of values compatible with Ford's view of industrial production. If adherence to these strict standards and values was a prerequisite to sharing in the profits, Ford promised in return not to fire workers except for unfaithfulness or inefficiency. Moreover, Ford supported this arrangement by establishing a committee to review all discharge cases and by providing a series of welfare activities (gymnasiums, programs of assistance for the families of workers in distress, and the like) geared to motivate workers and to free them of cares about home and family.

Men eagerly queued up at the factory gates, and turnover rates dropped rapidly in the wake of the Five Dollar Day. Labor hours per vehicle declined as well. But the pressures generated by the need for high-volume production and ever-lower costs took their toll. The policies and organizational structures needed to support this approach to work-force management could not be maintained, although the demands made on workers never decreased. When the commitment to such enlightened practices evaporates, as it did at Ford after World War I, benevolent paternalism can quite rapidly turn into heavy-handed authoritarianism, vigorous anti-unionism, and a reliance on the morally repugnant activities of the justly infamous Service Department.[22]

V

There is, then, a profound irony in the lackluster performance of American manufacturers when they are measured against the quality and productivity achievements of the Japanese counterparts. We seem not to have learned the appropriate lessons from Ford's pathbreaking work at Rouge River, and the Japanese did. What Toyota and Nissan and Toyo Kogyo have done by way of mastering the requirements of progressive production is nothing American firms could not have matched—had they not lost their way somehow, had they not lost the thread. This is not to suggest that Japanese production systems are problem-free (more on this in the next chapter). It is only to say that we have been stubbornly resistant to learning from our own history, especially when that history is reflected back to us by an Asian culture half a world away.

Under the relentless pressures of competition, however, that resistance is at last beginning to crumble. Within the past few years American firms have undertaken a searching reassessment of their established ways of managing the work of production. This is no routine review. Competitive survival demanded that hard questions be asked, and they have been. The answers—generated in part by close study of Japanese practice—have not been filed in unread reports in forgotten desk drawers. They have already begun to effect fundamental changes in the way American firms manage production. Although Detroit has quite rightly refused to borrow wholesale from Japan or to give in to slavish imitation, it has studied Japanese accomplishments as a means for rethinking many of its own approaches.

With inventory, for example, the automobile producers have started to move away from the old "just-in-case" system toward a leaner, far more carefully controlled "just-in-time" system. GM has introduced new policies on stockpiling and on the scheduling of parts production at its multi-plant complexes in Flint and Pontiac, Michigan. These initiatives, along with better and more frequent communication, have led to significant reductions in work-in-process inventories. At Buick's Flint operations, production levels have remained roughly constant, but inventories have fallen overall by more than 40 percent during the past three years. In some assembly operations at Flint, moreover, the record has been even better: inventories reduced by a factor of ten. The point, of course, is not that one or another GM facility has made signal advances; such accomplishments as these are sprinkled throughout the industry. The point is that a new commitment to excellence in manufacturing has begun to make itself felt.

This emerging commitment is reflected as well in the closer linkages now being developed between producers and suppliers in the scheduling of parts shipments, in product design, and in quality. Where suppliers are located in close proximity to the plants, they have even been integrated into the manufacturers' daily production schedules—that is, they receive daily information from the relevant plants and make daily deliveries of parts. This type of arrangement—especially when coupled with the establishment of long-term contracts that give a supplier full responsibility for the design, engineering, production, and delivery of an entire vehicle system—makes the supplier far more a part of the team than, as was the case in the recent past, an outside vendor. The guiding principle is once again what it was during the evolution of the American manufacturing system in the nineteenth century: do not play suppliers off against each other in order to beat them down on price (although price remains important), but capitalize, where possible, on their technical strengths and on the greater commitment to product quality that comes with enhanced responsibility, a more timely exchange of information, and a long-term relationship.

These efforts to integrate suppliers into the work of production reflect a growing recognition of the importance of component parts to overall product quality, but they also reflect the heightened emphasis that improvement in quality now receives from management. Throughout the industry the old attitude of "inspect and repair" is moving toward an attitude of "get it right the first time." At Ford, for example, the advertising slogan "Quality is Job 1" accurately represents the attention being given to building quality into the final product at every stage of its development, fabrication, and assembly. Indeed, Ford now treats quality as a total system problem that requires the attention of appropriately trained personnel in many functional areas—personnel who can communicate with each other to identify and solve problems through, for example, shared concepts of statistical quality control.

In the management of quality, inventory, and supplier relations, what happens on the factory floor is critical—not because that is where all problems arise or all solutions get found but because in the automobile industry, as in American manufacturing generally, poor workforce management has in the past crippled even the most dedicated efforts to master production. Integrating people into the manufacturing process so that their skills and abilities become and *remain* a point of competitive leverage was the one great task that ultimately remained beyond the scope of Henry Ford's achievements during the early part of the century. None of his successors have done a consistently better job of it. Reaching this sixth stage of manufacturing development has eluded all those mass production industries on which the nation's economic health has long rested. Here, if anywhere, remains the central unmet challenge of American manufacturing, and here remains one of its greatest opportunities to regain international competitiveness.

Chapter 7

Managing the
Human Resource

NO MATTER what the simpler-minded pundits might claim, American industry cannot regain its competitive vigor by striving to emulate all things Japanese. Differences in culture and macroeconomic environment are too great to allow successful knee-jerk imitation—even if it were desirable on other grounds, which it is not. The modern Japanese system of production is not some manufacturing Nirvana, free of all the tensions and problems that beset such systems elsewhere. It is the result of a set of deliberate choices and trade-offs and is appropriate not to every economic context imaginable but, rather, to the specific context of postwar Japan. If that country's social or political stability becomes problematical, if the work force ages too greatly, if expectations about living standards rise too quickly, if key industries cannot sustain their rate of growth, if—in short—changing conditions give the lie to the assumptions on which much of that production system rests, it will inevitably show the strain.

This is only another way of saying that what American industry has to learn from the Japanese is not to be learned through inflating the value of their example. The proper lesson is of a different sort. What the Japanese have done is to build an approach to the work of manufacturing that takes explicitly and centrally into account the realities of the new industrial competition. By contrast, American managers too often view their work through a haze of outdated assumptions and expectations. Like weary jet travellers whose inner clocks signal bedtime when the business day is at its height, they remain overly faithful to the old rules of thumb, the old nostrums, the old formulas. "We are going to invest X billion dollars over Y years," they say. "When the market improves and the volume comes back, we'll be in fine shape." Dollars and volume, however, no longer cure everything.

Today competition demands careful mastery of the guts, the nuts and bolts, of manufacturing operations. Resources heaped on those operations from without may be useful, even essential, but it is the close, detailed management of production systems themselves that determines success or failure. More particularly, it is the coordination of equipment, materials, and human resources that counts.

How tasks are assigned, responsibilities developed, and roles defined has a profound influence on all aspects of a company's operations. Organizational design, plant layout, systems of quality control, and a host of other considerations are but empty shells until given life by the skills, relationships, expectations, and capacity for learning embodied in the work force. This reservoir of human talent and adaptability is a long-lived asset, which like all such assets requires constant investment and careful nurturing. Unlike other assets, however, it is the primary determinant of what a company can or cannot do over the long run—that is, of a company's ability to respond to change. Without human strengths, new machinery, advanced techniques, and elaborate strategies are not worth a farthing. If the reservoir is allowed to run dry, no sudden burst of management attention can set things to rights. Bare survival may be possible, at least for a while, but response to change (the hallmark of industrial vitality) is not.

In the Japanese factories we visited, the labor force was an essential part of the production system. Although workers functioned under conditions of stress (remember, under the "rule of Kanban" low inventory levels constantly expose problems and create social as well as organizational pressures to solve them), the allocation of stress was generally fair. Equally important, the necessary means for accomplishing their tasks lay within the workers' own hands. They were not held responsible for a quality of performance about which they could in practice do nothing. As one of our colleagues has observed, the esprit de corps, teamwork, training, cool-headed performance under pressure, and commitment to a common goal that characterize Japanese workers resemble nothing so much in the West as the operation of a first-class pit crew during the Indianapolis 500.[1]

Only when management holds up its end—supplying the right equipment and training, instilling the right values, compensating crew members appropriately, setting achievable but difficult goals, relying on team members for advice and insight—can the crew do its work effectively. So, too, in the factory setting. Managers cannot simply wish a talented and dedicated labor force into being.

85

They must reinforce with their own policies and actions the allocation of responsibility well down in the organization. They cannot, as some current faddists would have it, shortcut the process by imposing quality circles and the like from the top.[2] First comes the deliberate nurturing of conditions under which teamwork and problem-solving can flourish; then and only then comes the apparatus of formal quality circles.

But when that seed is planted on well-prepared soil, the results can be astounding. Early one morning at Toyota's Takaoka assembly plant, for example, we attended a meeting of a seven-man quality circle from the plant's trim line. The White Eagles, as they called themselves, had just come off the night shift but quickly turned their attention to the same problem on which they had been working for a number of months. The problem: of the 10,000 vehicles produced each month, 7 had incorrectly mounted door gaskets (the rubber seals into which the doors fit in order to make an airtight closure). By changing their job layout, the group had already reduced the number of models on which they erred to 1, a cold-weather model that required a special gasket. For forty-five minutes the White Eagles discussed the best way to rid themselves of this last error. Would it help to relocate the job ticket from the end of the car to the side where the gasket was to be mounted? Should they approach the workers who affixed the ticket to see if such relocation were possible?

More interesting, perhaps, than the earnestness of the conversation was the process by which the group had decided upon the problem to study. On their own initiative they had gone to the quality control group at the end of the trim line and asked about the most frequent type of defect that originated in their area. As we noted above, this kind of self-starting and self-implementing teamwork cannot be bought for cash on the barrelhead. It is possible only when managers seriously and consistently take it as their own job to create the environment within which such group activity can thrive.

II

It is no accident that such an environment is not common today in the American automobile industry, for the sorry position of the labor force in that industry has a long history. As the work of building a car became increasingly standardized and as hierarchical bureaucracies sprang up to control the complexity wrought by standardization, the individual craftsmen of the industry's earliest years gave way to legions of wage-earners hemmed in by a thicket of rules, procedures, management suspicion, and constant supervision. At Ford, for example, members of the Service Department, which was created by Harry Bennett, took supervision to excessive lengths and often functioned like an in-plant police force, patrolling the aisles and phoning in regular reports.[3] When unionization became a heated issue during the 1930s, servicemen were even used to break up lunch conversations among workers, identify union sympathizers, harass or intimidate those suspected of union activities, and—as in the infamous "battle of the overpass" outside the Rouge complex in 1937—beat them up.

Ford was not alone. At General Motors, Pinkerton agents infiltrated union meetings and kept their leaders under surveillance.[4] The point, however, is not that American producers were guilty of this or that infringement of what later came to be regarded as workers' rights but that—long before collective bargaining put it all in writing—the relations between managers and workers had become one of deep mutual antagonism and distrust. Leaders and subordinates on both sides were committed to what they all saw as a bitter struggle, and the inevitable acts of violence and illegality made it only more bitter still.

No doubt fears about the radical changes that might follow recognition of the union helped polarize management's attitude, but then some of what the union wanted was radical indeed—a thirty-hour week and joint union-management control over line speeds.[5] There was also, of course, the ever-present threat of a major strike, such as that at GM in 1937, to dissuade those in power from voluntarily giving over their prerogatives and to encourage them to interpret any call to do so as a call to battle. Writing to GM employees in January, 1937, Alfred Sloan put the issue in this (not exactly moderate) way:

> Will a labor organization run the plants of General Motors Corporation or will the management continue to do so? On this issue depends the question as to whether you have to have a union card to hold a job, or whether your job will depend in the future, as it has in the past, upon your own . . . merit.
>
> In other words, will you pay tribute to a private group of labor dictators for the privilege of working or will you have the right to work as you may desire? Wages, working conditions, honest collective bargaining, have little, if anything, to do with the underlying situation. They are simply a smoke screen to cover the real objective.[6]

And that objective? To impose a dictatorship on individual citizens in their economic lives no less binding than that imposed by the European dictatorships of the same era on citizens in their political lives. Or so the impassioned rhetoric of the time would have it. It is no wonder that, in the 1941 representation election at Ford, only 5 percent of the work force voted with the company. Nor is it any wonder that the first real impact of the union after recognition (GM had recognized the United Auto Workers in 1937) was not on wages directly but, rather, on the processes by which wages and conditions of employment were set and administered—the formal negotiation and grievance procedures that would become so common in later years.

These new procedures prepared the way, though they certainly did not guarantee, union involvement in production-related decisions, and it was this possibility that by instinct management opposed most strongly. Nowhere was the participation of labor in such decisions genuinely thought of as a desirable objective—save, of course, by labor itself. In the particular circumstances of individual plants, unions did over time gain a voice in production matters, but each of these situations was highly idiosyncratic. For the most part, neither labor nor management behaved especially well, and neither saw the other as a valued partner in a necessarily joint effort.

Where irresponsibility on the one side meets weakness or confusion on the other, bizarre arrangements are bound to develop. Consider, for example, the following description of the state of affairs at Nash-Kelvinator's main plant in the late 1940s:

There was a men's barbershop in the men's room operated by company employees on company time with company pay. Workers had taken company parts and made electric ranges and refrigerators for the restroom. One woman was cooking breakfast for five men every morning after they got to work as a small scale restaurant business. . . . One employee bagged a bear during the hunting season and roasted cuts of it in the big ovens used to bake moisture out of the compressors. Poker games . . . flourished. The men were literally working only half the time they were paid, and had come to regard the situation as legitimate. One day a worker was hurt in a plant accident at 10 A.M. The rules provided that any worker who had to go home before noon because of injury should get a half day's pay. The man, however, demanded and received a full day's pay because between 7 and 10 A.M. he had already done a day's work by plant standards.[7]

For out-of-control nonsense like this, both union and management are surely to blame, but for both sides neither the heritage of adversarial relations nor the absurd practices to which they often give rise are easy to overcome. When labor views management as inept and gullible, it will run restaurants in a men's room; when managers view workers as incompetent malingerers, they will treat them as an enemy to be appeased or an opponent to be tricked but never as a partner to be taken seriously, listened to, and employed sensibly.

No company can richly value the potential of its labor force as a competitive asset when a high-ranking officer (here John Scoville, chief economist of Chrysler in the 1940s) can observe in all seriousness, "While I condemn collective bargaining as an assault on liberty, as an evil thing which is against the public interest, as something which will increase poverty, I realize that collective bargaining is only one chick in the whole brood of vultures that seek to pick the meat from the bones of honest men. . . ."[8] For years, however, sentiments like these were—if not the pinnacle—then at least the tableland of moderation in the automobile industry.

During the 1950s Chrysler and Ford both determined—though for quite different reasons—to emulate the labor policies of GM, which had been the first company in the industry to adopt a thoroughly business-like approach to union-related matters.[9] (Chrysler's main concern was to improve the rather lax efficiency of its plants; Ford's to improve the markedly inept administration of contract provisions at the local level.) But the model these companies chose to follow was, for all of its contribution to GM's market success, still an effort to preserve managerial prerogative at virtually any cost. Even if GM's intention was not to "get" the union but only to do what was objectively "best for business," nonetheless its strict and clear assignments at all organizational levels bespoke a negotiating stance that was at the time widely regarded as tough, pragmatic, shrewd, and distinctly "old pro." No less than Ford or Chrysler, GM viewed the UAW as an adversary; sooner than Ford or Chrysler, however, it accepted the UAW as an inevitable fact of life to be dealt with firmly but consistently.

In practice, GM's approach resulted in relatively efficient plants, few major work stoppages or local strikes, and a host of minor skirmishes at the bargaining table as well as on the shop floor. There was no management-union harmony, only a cease fire. There was no genuinely cooperative relationship, only an armed truce. Blue-collar employees enjoyed better pay and working conditions than they had a generation before, but the nature of their work had changed little. Jobs remained narrow in scope, with few opportunities for involvement or responsibility or initiative. Control of production remained a function of machine speeds, watchful supervision, work standards, and measurement techniques. By the mid-1950s collective bargaining had changed a number of operational procedures, but it had not changed the long-established paradigm of production. The press to meet production targets, delivery schedules, and efficient volume levels drove the system much as it had a decade or two or three previously.

Throughout this period, however, both sides made out quite well. Profits grew, and so did compensation levels; for as Walter Reuther reminded his listeners, "Our job is to cut the fat off." Beyond just adding dollars to the paycheck, moreover, the UAW and the auto producers led the way in pension arrangements, health and welfare benefits, cost-of-living adjustments, and the like. High market demand for American-built cars—especially when combined with minimal competition from abroad—cushioned the sharp edges of the uneasy truce between management and labor. Record levels of production and an above-average rate of output per work hour hid a multitude of sins.

THE CASE OF THE AUTOMOBILE INDUSTRY

Submission to the manufacturing paradigm may have been galling, but it paid well; the unions may have won substantial concessions, but new technology and capital equipment promised management renewed leverage over production. If this early version of détente was to prove inherently unstable, the forces that would shake it to its roots did not loom large on the horizon in the Eisenhower years.

But during the 1960s, danger signs began to appear in local plants and in the talk of local union officials. In preparation for national bargaining in 1961, GM's unions submitted over 19,000 demands for contract changes; in 1964, that number jumped to 24,000.[10] The rank and file was more restless than it had been in a generation: unexcused absences increased by 50 percent between 1965 and 1969, the number of grievances by 38 percent, disciplinary layoffs by 44 percent, turnover rates by 72 percent. A management policy of "paying a lot and keeping the heat on" no longer seemed as effective as it once had been; it might buy sullen acquiescence, but it could not buy worker loyalty or commitment. And when, in the early 1970s, workers at GM's highly-automated Lordstown plant erupted in a bitter dispute over line speeds and redesigned jobs, many observers thought they caught a glimpse of a future of newly acrimonious industrial relations.

Some managers had little trouble reading the handwriting on the wall. Others, by far the majority, were reluctant to acknowledge any direct or meaningful connection amongst labor unrest, productivity, and company performance. After all, did not the industry's history show that the best way to boost output and profits was to reassert managerial prerogative? As one foreman noted, "Let's face it. The only way to get things done is to get down on the floor and knock a few heads."[11] Knocking heads might not win management any friends on the shop floor, but who needed friends? Heavy-handed assertions of authority might not be fit material for family-hour television viewing, but who cared? The point was to keep the system working as it had in the past, for its dollars-and-cents record as a manufacturing paradigm was impressive.

In the 1980s, however, when measured against the performance of Japanese companies like Toyota or Nissan or Toyo Kogyo, that record has lost its appeal, for the Japanese have changed in a fundamental way the terms on which competition in the automobile industry must be carried out. The imperatives of quality and productivity, which lie at the heart of this new industrial competition, are impossible to satisfy without the active, loyal, and committed participation of a well-trained and constantly improving work force. In this new environment, what passed for an American labor-force policy in previous years is not only out of date; it is poison. It is not merely a curious relic of another era; it can be lethal to those who rely on it.

This is, of course, not to suggest that union relations in Japan are barren of friction. At Toyo Kogyo, for example, workers told us rather candidly that the union was essential to protect workers from capricious decisions by management and that management sometimes tries to force higher output rates from workers even when it has not made its investment contribution. Nonetheless, the narrow wage differential between managers and senior workers, the absence of status symbols that sharply differentiate managerial positions from those of blue-collar labor, and the fact that first-line supervisors, lower-level managers, engineers, salespeople, office workers, and other staff personnel are all union members—these conditions help make Japanese unions more like an arm of a company's personnel department than (as is the UAW) a steady, if sometimes cooperative, adversary.[12]

III

It is no accident, then, that work-force management in America has developed the way it has. The gradual evolution of a single, dominant paradigm for production and, for much of this century, the success it has enjoyed in the market have driven home to many managers the apparent validity of the assumptions upon which that paradigm was based. If skills can be progressively built into machines, then workers need not be especially skilled themselves. If a production system is to run economically, all considerations must be subordinated to the achievement of continuous high-volume operations. If costs creep up too far, turn up the pressure on workers or cut their pay or both. In short, follow the gospel of "volume above all else" with an unblinking faith in its ultimate rightness, get skilled people out of the system wherever possible, automate everything in sight, gear up for long production runs, buffer yourself with enough inventory to keep the lines moving, inspect for defects—if at all—at the end of those lines, treat workers primarily as a reservoir of costs that can be bled out under pressure as the need arises, and you will boost your market share, your profits, your stockholders' good disposition, your bond ratings, your own compensation, and the nation's industrial health.

All that this managerial siren song lacked was the distant strains of a heavenly choir, but on a clear night in corporate America one could almost hear the angels at their instruments. For a half century and more, this gospel has been the home remedy of choice for American industry. It was guaranteed to do everything but cure the common cold and, perhaps, even that too. Hallelujahs and heavenly music notwithstanding, as a patent medicine, it was pure snake oil. Complex machines require more not less highly skilled operators, even if what it means to operate a machine is rapidly changing. A premium on efficiency places greater not lesser importance on machine uptime and on the many incremental improvements by which operators coax the best performance out of their specialized equipment. Building good quality products is impossible without the active cooperation of a dedicated and talented labor force. If this gospel were ever true, it is true no longer, and some American managers have finally begun to work themselves free of its pernicious influence.

Imagine an American plant with no executive parking or dining areas, no general foremen, relatively few support staff, no multi-classification systems for job descriptions and compensation, workers (all union members) divided into teams with responsibility for production, quality control, materials handling, and the like. Further, imagine the whole had been planned by a committee on which sat four union members as active participants. A figment of the imagination? Not at all. It is the Cadillac engine plant in Livonia, Michigan, which along with many other facilities is rapidly demonstrating that a new American paradigm for production is indeed possible at the level of work-force management.

Working with the director of Organizational Research and Development in GM's personnel department and his staff, a small number of middle managers began in the early 1970s to experiment with the linkages between human relations and job satisfaction, on the one hand, and various measures of production (meeting delivery schedules, keeping costs down, and so on), on the other. The task forces, committees, and participation groups they established (or encouraged) with the help of local officials began to show positive results by the mid-1970s: in some plants grievances dropped, absences declined, quality improved, and changeover times shortened.

These joint efforts did not appear out of the blue; they had been made possible by the letter of understanding that GM signed with the UAW to set up a "Committee to Improve the Quality of Work Life," which in turn legitimized the involvement of UAW leaders in a host of different QWL (Quality of Work Life) programs at the grass roots level.[13] Important figures on both sides balked at these new arrangements, but several carried forward the effort with missionary zeal and slowly began to silence their critics not by assertions of authority but by the inescapable fact of their achievements.

At this writing, to be sure, a new orientation toward work-force management has not completely replaced older attitudes throughout the GM organization or that of Ford or Chrysler. Nor is there any formal master plan about what such an approach must or should include. For some participants, it means better communication skills; for others, more worker involvement in the planning or improvement of production operations. For all, however, it means a concerted attempt to view the work force as an essential point of lever-age for competitive success against foreign producers. In 1979, GM's Executive Vice-President for North American Automotive Operations made participation in some kind of QWL program mandatory for all of GM's plants, the choice of approach being left to local preference. At the time, there could have been no stronger signal that management, at the top level at least, finally understood just how valuable a strategic asset its work force was.

GM, we hasten to point out, has not had a private revelation. The other major domestic firms have also begun to face up to the same competitive realities. At Ford, for example, the support and involvement of the UAW Vice-President helped push forward the establishment of an Employee Involvement Program at half the company's U.S. facilities in a rather short period of time. If GM's efforts were more varied and far-reaching in some situations, Ford's were more focused, uniform, and broadly based, including a major attempt to redefine the union-company relationship. Through careful attention to outdated contract provisions, to processes for on-going joint consultation, and to the promotion of training, Ford sought to break down the barriers of suspicion and contempt that had grown up between workers and management. By placing the responsibility for action on those people who have the best information no matter what their titles and by seeking to foster the more effective integration of workers into all aspects of the manufacturing process, Ford hoped to lay a new foundation for excellence in manufacturing.

The record of success for programs like these is not unmixed. Where implemented, they have not always worked well; where involved, not all managers have been convinced that these new initiatives are worthwhile. Still trapped by their old view of the world, some top-level managers have even seen them as a heaven-sent opportunity to get workers to drop their objections to stricter work standards, faster line speeds, and heightened managerial control. But it is not a legitimate criticism of these efforts to fault them for the possibility that they might be misused. If that logic were sound, we ought as well deny the value of some important new medicine because individual doctors might not prescribe it accurately. Let us be frank. As in any long-standing feud, some members on both sides will turn whatever comes to hand against their sworn enemies. But in this industrial version of the Hatfields and the McCoys, mutual intransigence is no longer acceptable as a principle of survival. In the face of stiff foreign competition, it is a blueprint for extinction. Brute self-interest, not the hymns to good fellowship of pious onlookers, dictates entente—if not cordial, then at least cooperative. And, as our research has shown, improved work-force management can indeed have a catalytic effect on the overall quality of manufacturing operations, even in older plants where a history of bad feelings and lackluster performance is deeply entrenched.

Although the capacity for significant improvement certainly exists, the persistence of antediluvian attitudes can render it stillborn. For example, during negotiations for the GM-UAW contract finally agreed to in March, 1982, GM's Chairman lambasted the UAW's leaders for "stamped[ing] this herd of buffalo [the workers] by telling them they're underpaid. Now they've got to tell them that they're overpaid in relation to the competition."[14] Not to be outdone, the UAW blasted GM's suggestion that data on relative cost and quality levels be made available to the work force, arguing that QWL "was never intended to be a vehicle to propagandize or parrot the current views of the Chairman of the board of GM as to how to serve General Motors through worker sacrifice."[15]

The rhetoric here is catchy enough and fondly reminiscent of old battle lines. It may well serve as a powerful reminder that strong forces—organizational, ideological, procedural, intellectual—stand in the way of necessary change. As always, however, it is the task of leaders to see beyond the inherited passions of the moment to the requirements of long-term interests. In business as in politics, there is no trick to waving the bloody shirt of long-standing grievance, nothing particularly difficult about paralyzing a society's or an organization's determination to excel. By contrast, the imperatives of courage, vision, and high position argue for the harder course: putting aside destructive animosity and outdated practice to build better for the future. Without such leadership and faced with the new industrial competition, American industry will all too easily find itself in that awful, unredeemable state of limbo described by Matthew Arnold, "Wandering between two worlds; one dead/ The other unable to be born."

PART III

The Possibilities
of De-Maturity

IN the last three chapters of the book, we further develop and test our conceptual framework for understanding the ways in which technical change affects competition at different stages of industry evolution. Here, as earlier, we are well aware how easily discussions of technology can fail to distinguish between some measure of an innovation's technical novelty and some measure of its effects on established production competence. We have tried to be consistent in defining as "radical" those innovations that represent a substantial degree of novelty; and as "minor" or "modest" those innovations that are of lesser novelty. Similarly, we have defined as "conservative" innovations whose effect is to extend or refine existing design concepts or production systems; and as "disruptive" those innovations whose effect is to destroy such concepts or systems. Further, we have reserved the term "incremental" for technical activities of a conservative nature where the work of refinement or extension (whatever its novelty) proceeds by gradual steps; and the term "epochal" for activities of a disruptive nature where the disruption (whatever its novelty) is substantial.

Now, it often happens that minor innovations are conservative. But this need not be the case. During some phases of industry evolution—de-maturity, for example—changes of little technical novelty may have an immense effect on established modes of doing business. Keeping issues of novelty separate from issues of production competence is important. So, too, is keeping this latter concern distinct from issues of market linkages. The work of conservation, as of disruption, can unequally affect design concepts and production systems, on the one hand, and market linkages, on the other. That is, a disruptive innovation may cause a great upheaval in an industry's production system without overturning such established linkages as distribution channels and the like. Or it may upset those linkages while leaving the production system intact. We need, then, a term for describing the overall competitive impact of an innovation, no matter how its influence is distributed. For this usage we have adopted the term "transilience," which we explain and illustrate in chapter 9 and, again, in appendix D.

These problems of language are anything but trivial, for they provide a reliable guide to the three axes of interpretation along which the significance of an innovation will fall: technical novelty, effects on production systems, and effects on market linkages. These axes, in turn, allow us to translate with increased precision from the domain of technical activity to the domain of industry competition. When we argue, as we do in the following chapters, that the automobile industry is undergoing a process of de-maturity, being able to distinguish the various competitive effects of innovation as well as the developments whose source lies elsewhere is of considerable value. Not least, it allows us to define with greater accuracy what we mean by de-maturity.

In the automobile industry, foreign producers with manufacturing systems geared to high quality and low cost production have created competitive pressures on Detroit that reinforce, but are not identical to, the pressures generated by the gradual breaking down of long-established linkages between design concepts and market preferences. It is this combination of technology- and production-driven adjustments that distinguishes the industry's movement toward de-maturity—adjustments that are slowly becoming visible in new approaches to manufacturing management, new product and process technology, experimentation with new design concepts, and so on.

These developments do not, of course, reliably mirror developments in any other industry. In an important sense, they are unique to the historical circumstances of automobile production and marketing. Even so, we have tried to construct a way of thinking about de-maturity that views it as but one of many possible forms that a renewed production- and/or technology-driven competition might take. It is not the only one, nor is it necessarily the most common. It may be that de-maturity—especially de-maturity in the automobile industry—gives us only a single window through which to view the new terms of competition, but a discerning look through that window can help make us aware of the range of possibilities in the wider landscape of industry evolution.

Chapter 8

De-Maturity and the Change in Market Preference

UNDER the pressure of certain competitive realities, the seemingly inevitable movement of productive units toward maturity can reverse itself. In theory, at least, this kind of reversal is possible. It can happen. Whether it is happening in, for example, the automobile industry is of course another question entirely.

If de-maturity is, indeed, in progress, we know from chapter 2 that technology will return as a centrally important aspect of competition. The demand side of the market will require the satisfaction of a new cluster of needs and preferences; the supply side will experiment with new dimensions of performance and value. As a result, this mutual search process will make technology more *visible* (innovations will strike at more apparent aspects of product function; consumers will be intentionally looking for new ways to meet their demands), more *valuable* (either in terms of a price premium or of enhanced market share), and more *diverse* (the process of search will spawn a variety of efforts). By itself, however, even a sustained growth in technological visibility, value, and diversity does not inevitably point toward de-maturity: to do so, it must also be achievable only through the destruction and replacement of existing production competence.

When innovation is, at best, limited in its effects on manufacturing processes, industry structure and modes of competition need undergo little adjustment. When, by contrast, technical ferment in the market necessitates major alterations in production systems, then innovation can restructure an industry. Thus, if we want to know whether de-maturity is really happening, we must ask, first, whether the overall importance attached to technology by the market is increasing and, then, whether this heightened importance threatens production competence.

II

It is no easy matter to ascertain the appeal of technology to the market. One reasonable way to begin is to survey the advertisements placed in various media by automobile producers, for the product characteristics that receive the most attention may serve as a useful indication of what producers think the market wants.[1] Some observers, it is true, view modern reliance on advertising as, at best, distasteful and, at worst, disturbingly manipulative.[2] Nonetheless, advertisements do reflect reasoned (if not always accurate) judgments about the factors that enter into consumers' buying decisions and, in particular, about those bits of information that can persuade consumers to act.

Thus, without pushing the case too far, we would argue that, if technology has indeed become more visible in the market for automobiles, advertisements should show as much. To check our assumption, we have analyzed several hundred magazine advertisements for automobiles for the period 1961–1981 (see appendix C for details). We report our results in figure 8.1.

We considered four classes of product characteristics (luxury/styling, performance, economy—including purchase price and operating and repair costs—and technology), but our focus was on technology. As the figure shows, the emphasis placed on domestic car technology rose dramatically in 1980 and 1981, even though changes in the nature and focus of innovative effort had already been in process for quite some time. Still, the 1980–1981 data are striking. Between 1961 and 1979, U.S. producers gave little space in their advertisements to technological matters; styling and luxury dominated advertising messages. The catalytic effects of the 1979 oil shock, however, so greatly accelerated the coming to fruition of the renewed technological emphasis among U.S. producers that they quickly surpassed the efforts of foreign producers, who for their part had been technology-oriented (at least in relative terms) all along. Evidence cited in appendix C shows further that economy of operation also became a dominant theme in the late 1970s and, along with technology, replaced styling and performance as items of central concern.

100

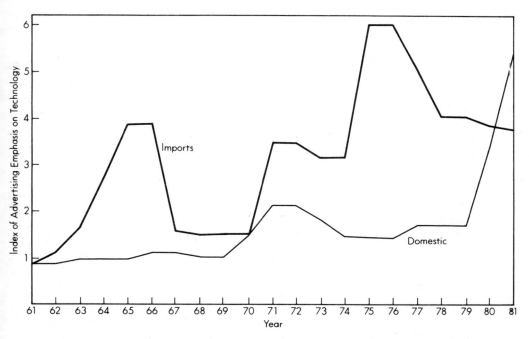

Figure 8.1 *Trends in Automobile Advertising Emphasis on Technology 1961–1981*
Domestic versus Imports

SOURCE: See appendix to chapter 8.

NOTE: The index of advertising emphasis is a measure of how important technology was in
the message of advertisements in a given year. The appendix contains details.

These advertising data are certainly not conclusive evidence, but they are
suggestive. The messages deliberately sent by manufacturers to consumers follow the pattern we would expect them to follow if, as our model of de-maturity
postulates, technology were taking on greater competitive importance in the
market. Figure 8.1 leaves small room for doubt that technology has indeed
become more competitively visible than it was twenty years ago. But this is
only half the story. When consumers actually step into a dealer's showroom
and plunk down their hard-earned dollars, are they more willing than they
used to be to pay a premium for new technology? Does heightened visibility
translate into a market premium for innovation?

To answer this question, we have estimated the market valuation of a few
representative product characteristics both before and after the oil shock of
1979. But even more than our work with advertising data, these calculations
involve subtle methodological issues. No market exists for individual characteristics as such, although it is possible to look on the total price of a vehicle
as the sum of the implicit prices for the bundle of attributes that comprise it.[3]

101

Still, these implicit prices are hard to get at and can be determined only indirectly. If, for example, a Buick Regal sells for $10,000 when equipped with a turbocharger and for $9350 without, we may infer that the turbocharger's market price is $650. In most cases, however, the relevant comparisons are not so readily available and must be constructed through various statistical operations.[4]

Our approach, therefore, requires accurate information both on product characteristics and on the prices that buyers actually pay—not on the suggested retail prices listed by manufacturers. Since transaction prices for new cars are not readily available, we have used "year later" prices as determined by the used car market, but we have also taken into account the effect of a model's initial list price on its year later price. (Again, the details of our method are given in appendix C.) Our purpose here is to derive an estimate of the market premium (or discount) relative to list price that is associated with given technological features. Accordingly, we have compared prices of several features—engine type (gas or diesel), drive train (front or rear wheel), package efficiency (the relation between interior volume and weight), fuel efficiency, driving range, and model age (as a general measure of technical newness)—in the 1977–1978 period (before the 1979 oil shock) with their prices in the 1979–1980 period. Our results are summarized in table 8.1.

The question, remember, is whether technology has begun to carry a market

TABLE 8.1

*Estimated Market Premiums (and
Discounts) Before and After the Oil Shock of
1979*

Characteristics	1977–1978	1979–1980
Technology		
Diesel Engine	($853.0)	$301.7
Front-Wheel Drive	($315.0)	$416.0
Model Age	($ 11.3)	($ 36.8)
Other		
Miles per Gallon	$36.2	($14.0)
Driving Range	$ 0.1	$ 1.0
Package Efficiency	($ 8.1)	$ 3.4

SOURCE: See appendix B.
NOTE: The dollar values in the table are estimates of the premiums or discounts (discounts in parentheses) that consumers were willing to pay for a unit of the given characteristic, other things being equal. In the case of diesel engines and front-wheel drive, the "unit" of the characteristic is an all-or-nothing proposition—the dollar value is the premium (or discount) applied to the diesel engine (or front-wheel drive).

premium. As table 8.1 argues with but minor qualifications, the answer must be a resounding yes. Consider, for example, that with other things held constant (miles per gallon, driving range, and so on), a car with front-wheel drive would have sold for $315 less in the 1977–1978 used car market than would its rear-wheel drive counterpart. By contrast, in 1979–1980, that $315 discount would have turned into a $416 premium. Much the same, of course, is true for diesel engines (even with fuel efficiency and driving range held constant) and package efficiency. In short, during the late 1970s the market substantially and unmistakably changed the value it placed on certain technological features.[5]

Perhaps the clearest indication of this change in market valuation is the data on the effect of model age on transaction price. True, in both periods (other things held constant), the older the model the larger the discount, but the discount in 1979–1980 was significantly greater than in 1977–1978. Newness in and of itself attracted a premium in the later market that it simply did not enjoy in the earlier, which may simply be another way of saying that pre-1979 buyers were relatively indifferent to technological innovation. When innovation holds no direct appeal for buyers, the design continuity of older models gives them somewhat greater appeal, for buyers assume that they have been debugged and perfected. When innovation is prima facie attractive, the lure of new solutions to new clusters of buyer preference outweighs the appeal, however sanguine, of debugged perfection.

III

Neither the heightened value nor visibility of technology in the market, we must repeat, necessarily threatens production competence and thus leads toward industry de-maturity. To the contrary, a burst of technical ferment—even like that of the late 1970s—can represent no more than a short-lived transition from one dominant design to another. If there is no active search or learning on both sides of the market—that is, if the diversity of available technical options remains small and if few means exist to meet evolving consumer preferences—then the technical changes that do take place are likely to be merely incremental in nature. And as we have argued previously, incremental changes are characteristic of the mature state of industry development. Without a major increase in the diversity of technology, therefore, visibility and value are inconclusive as evidence for de-maturity.

The diversity of design concepts actually offered for sale in the market is,

103

then, something of a litmus test. We stress these "embodied" concepts because ideas still under development and not yet embodied in products available for sale cannot, by definition, be the objects of buyer acceptance or rejection. There is, however, another, more important reason for insisting on this kind of measure of diversity: it offers genuine assistance in the search for indications of de-maturity in process.

When a product is first introduced, diversity of product technology is fairly easy to spot, for differences among the several extant versions of the product will often reflect differences in core concepts. In the early years of the automobile industry, for example, no dominant approach emerged concerning the choice of fuel on which engines were supposed to run. One did not need a doctorate in advanced physics to observe the market diversity represented by steam cars, electric cars, and gasoline cars. But after design hierarchies have crystallized, it becomes increasingly difficult to observe technical diversity—not least because technical ferment typically appears first in the peripheral aspects of such hierarchies. Only as this ferment finally reaches a core concept—the exchange, say, of one basic principle of engine design for another—does it receive general attention. By looking only at core concepts, even our well-trained physicist can miss much of what is really going on. Thus, the existence of market search and experimentation with less central aspects of technology provides an early warning signal of potentially important activity well down on the design hierarchy. Diversity helps track the possibilities of de-maturity.

As a proxy for overall diversity in the automobile industry, we have used data on design concepts for the engines and drive trains of U.S.-produced vehicles between 1970 and 1980. The particular items we looked at are unglamorous and mundane: the number of cylinders in the engine, the type of fuel delivery (fuel injection or carburetion), the placement of valves and camshaft, the type of fuel (gas or diesel), the orientation of the engine (transverse or longitudinal), and the location of the drive (rear wheel or front). Our choice was deliberate. If technical diversity is really increasing, it ought to show up in product characteristics like these. Our decision to look at only U.S.-produced vehicles was deliberate as well. We wanted to distinguish between diversity that arose from the introduction of new design concepts in U.S.-produced automobiles and diversity that arose from a shift in product mix toward small imported cars.

Our approach here was to develop a measure of technological diversity—a diversity index, if you will—that was based on the market shares of different design concepts. For every relevant design parameter (the number of cylinders in an engine, say), the index will be highest—that is, show the greatest diversity—when the market shares of the various available configurations (in this case: four, six, or eight cylinders) are equal; lowest when one configuration holds 100 percent of the market. (Once again, for the details of our method, please see appendix C.) Our calculations, which are summarized in table 8.2, indicate quite clearly that the 1970s saw a marked increase in the diversity index of American-built cars.

More than 80 percent of all cars produced in the United States in 1970 had V-8 engines; all ran on gasoline; all had rear-wheel drive; none used fuel injection; and all had longitudinally mounted engines. By 1980, as table 8.2 demonstrates, these figures had radically changed. Not only that, these changes were not independent of each other. They tended, instead, to move through the market as clusters or "packages" of design concepts, each package including a particular combination of cylinders, engine orientation, drive train, and so on. Table 8.2 argues strongly that the absolute number of packages available in the market grew several times over during the 1970s. So, too, did their diversity index. Nor was this huge increase in diversity limited to the small car segment. At the end of the decade, the big jump took place among large cars. In the mid-size range, however, the dominance of V-6–engine-based packages by 1979–1980 actually reduced diversity.

On balance, then, without even looking to developments in electronics or new materials or engine computers or any of a host of other technical areas, we can see that the case for the substantially heightened diversity—as well as the visibility and value—of technology is inescapable. Thus, automobile pro-

TABLE 8.2

Diversity of Selected Engine/Drive-Train Packages (1970–1980)

Category	70	71	72	73	74	Year 75	76	77	78	79	80
I. Total Market											
Diversity Index	1.67	1.70	1.51	1.64	2.07	2.21	1.89	1.81	1.86	3.76	4.91
No. of Configurations	6	5	5	8	7	10	9	9	13	15	21
II. Market Segments											
Small Cars											
Diversity Index	1.82	2.59	2.02	2.38	2.34	2.17	2.95	2.94	3.55	3.54	3.64
No. of Configurations	5	4	3	6	6	6	6	6	8	9	11
Medium Cars											
Diversity Index	1.31	1.46	1.28	1.25	1.52	1.93	1.96	1.89	2.05	3.41	2.12
No. of Configurations	3	3	4	4	3	3	5	6	7	9	10
Large Cars											
Diversity Index	1.46	1.42	1.36	1.44	1.49	1.71	1.41	1.55	1.20	1.72	2.58
No. of Configurations	4	4	4	5	4	7	6	7	6	7	10

SOURCE: Calculated from data in appendix B.
NOTE: A configuration is a combination of engine type (fuel, number of cylinders, carburetion) and drive train (front or rear drive, engine orientation). The diversity index measures both the number of different configurations and their relative importance in the market. Small, medium, and large are defined in terms of weight, with breakpoints being 3,198 pounds and 3,660 pounds respectively.

ducers meet with ease all three of the market-related tests for an industry undergoing a process of de-maturity.

In the four preceding chapters we noted how the industry's long-established paradigm for production has recently been called into question. Here we have laid out the evidence for a concurrent breakdown in the fit between market preferences and design concepts. Together, these findings suggest rather strongly that the current ferment in the industry is not just a by-product of the usual thrust and parry of business rivalry. It is the outward sign of a production system being shaken to its foundations.

Chapter 9

De-Maturity and the

Competitive Significance

of Innovation

AS WE have argued in previous chapters, if an industry had indeed begun a process of de-maturity, we would expect to find important changes at work in its paradigm for production and in the value placed by its customers on technology. But we would also expect to find something else. If de-maturity is underway, we ought to be able to observe a subtle but competitively significant shift in the nature of innovative activity. Looking for the evidence of such a shift is an essential part of building the case for de-maturity, but it is something more as well. A change in the nature of innovation is both a sign of de-maturity in process and, in competitive terms, its most far-reaching effect.

When, for example, an industry reaches its mature phase of development, innovative activity tends to be, in technical terms, relatively minor, a matter of tinkering with processes which represent substantial investments of capital and human skill. Although tinkering of this sort may prove valuable in the marketplace, it has, by definition, little effect on the chosen means by which an industry or a company competes. It offers little threat to on-line production competence, but, in fact, extends and strengthens that competence—that is, it conserves design concepts already in place. This conservative effect, in turn, allows a company to do better what it currently does, not to do something entirely different.

There is, of course, the additional fact that in mature industries minor technical changes are readily imitable. When new skills are embodied in equipment that is available for purchase by competitors, they do not easily become the foundation of long-lasting market ascendancy. For all intents and purposes, technically modest innovations in mature industries are relatively neutral in their effect on the terms of competition, if not on market success. When, however, we try to think of innovations that are likely to alter those terms, almost inevitably we think of advances in fields like genetic engineering or semiconductor chips or telecommunications—that is, we look to radically new products and markets based on important scientific breakthroughs.

Nor are we alone in this knee-jerk response. The nation's overall experience with technology since World War II reinforces a general view that competitively significant innovation is something altogether novel. From the frontiers of work in solid-state physics, biochemistry, and other such disciplines have repeatedly come technological marvels that rendered old products obsolete, old industry boundaries irrelevant, and old modes of competition passé. If modest technical change is relatively powerless to change the industrial landscape, spectacular innovation can change it overnight. This, at least, has been the most obvious lesson of the past thirty years.

But there has been another lesson as well, one much harder to see and more difficult to grasp: the neutrality of minor technical change is, to be sure, a fact of life—but only under conditions of maturity. If, however, de-maturity sets in, even modest activity can have a disruptive (not conservative) effect on production competence and thus on competition.

The common mistake has been to equate relationships that are true under certain conditions with relationships that are true under all conditions. Confusing the contingent with the universal is an easy error to make, especially when one's experience has been entirely with the contingent. Merely because our sun rises every morning does not mean that all suns do, yet we are so used to the relationship that we take it for granted—not just as a description of our own experience but as a general truth about suns and mornings.

In an important sense, then, what we think we know from experience about innovation is not so much inaccurate as incomplete. So fixed are our expectations about the technical novelty of competitively significant innovations that we are often in the position of a conscientious homeowner who, fearing the dramatic danger posed by tornadoes, watches the sky incessantly while ignoring the enlarging cracks in the house's foundation. As a rule, we are so determined to see evidence of great technological novelty before we are willing to think of an innovation's potential effects on both production competence and competition that we forget that our industrial tornado-watch is appropriate to some, but not all, weather conditions.

We forget, as well, in our fascination with the sheer power of some innovations just how it is that they work their influence on free-standing industrial structures. Radical innovation alters the terms of competition in mature industries by upsetting established modes of production and by destroying existing linkages between design concepts and market preferences. In other words, the competitive significance of such innovations depends on their effects on markets and manufacturing systems. And this, of course, is also true for modest changes—the cracks in the foundation—under conditions of de-maturity.

For those observers who persist in equating technical novelty with competitive significance, the shift from rear- to front-wheel drive in the automobile industry signifies, at most, a quick hop from the rigidity of one dominant design to that of another, a transition with no more lasting competitive significance than the introduction of leather upholstery. For those who understand the logic of de-maturity, the shift in drive train is as destructive to entrenched competence as any tornado on the Kansas plains. Only the appearance in Detroit of a nuclear-powered hovercraft would convince the former group that massive competitive change was in the air; the latter see the threat posed by cracks in the foundation.

We exaggerate, but only by a little. What is truly important about innovation, whatever its technical novelty, is the extent to which it changes an industry's basis of competition at the same time that it disrupts established production competence, marketing and distribution systems, capital equipment, organizational structures, and the skills of both managers and workers. In a mature industry, innovation is usually conservative, reinforcing the terms of competition. By contrast, in a de-maturing industry, even technically modest innovations can throw competitive logic and the nature of essential resources to the wind. Technology affects competition only to the extent that it—and in the way that it—supports or threatens existing commitments: to production systems, to tactical plans and strategic goals, and to the use of resources.

II

An industry's structure (the relative position of established firms), basis of competition (the dimensions of product and process among which those firms seek to differentiate themselves so as to obtain advantage), and nature of resources (the whole gamut of competencies, individual and institutional, needed to compete successfully) are all influenced to some degree by technical change. The question is how and how much. In other words, the question concerns the nature and extent of an innovation's "transilience"—that is, its capacity to influence production systems and their linkages with the market. To talk about the competitive effects of technology, then, is to talk about its transilience.

The degree of transilience implicit in a given innovation is a measure of that innovation's disruption of production systems and market linkages. Figure 9.1 presents a scheme for visualizing the different degrees of the transilience of innovation. Along the horizontal axis, innovations are classified in terms of their capacity to influence production systems: changes that conserve existing designs are found to the left of the midpoint; those that disrupt them, to the right. Along the vertical axis, innovations are classified by their effects on market linkages: above the midpoint are technical changes that either create new markets or new channels of distribution, or alter old ones; below the midpoint, changes that maintain or reinforce current market linkages. The four quadrants graphed by this simple matrix offer more than a handy method of categorization; they correspond rather closely to the state of affairs most common at different stages of process/product evolution. What the matrix permits, then, is a dynamic analysis of how transilience itself shifts over time.

In the upper right-hand quadrant fall those epochal innovations whose effect is to create entirely new design concepts and, more important, the production systems and markets to accommodate them. Because these changes in technology tend to occur early on, address fundamental characteristics of product and process, and establish design hierarchies that set the agenda for later develop-

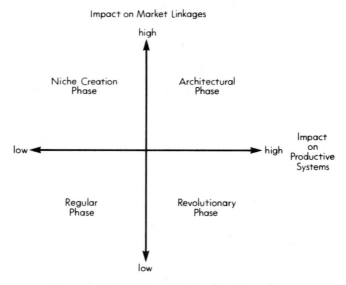

Figure 9.1 *Evolution of Technology Transilience*

ments, we have chosen to label them "architectural" innovations. Much as the foundation of a building defines the broad structural limits that the upper floors must respect (but not, for example, the placement of non-load-bearing walls or the style of exterior decoration), an architectural innovation—like the laser, or the computer, or the handheld electronic calculator—defines a large, but not infinite, range of possibilities for markets and production systems.

The more these architectural innovations require substantial change in existing organizational commitments and competence, the more obvious their transilience. When they fall on virgin ground, as they commonly do, their transilience is not diminished, although it can be harder to see. The competitive effects of technical changes are most readily visible when they meet and overcome resistance. It is usually the case, however, that architectural innovation occurs during that stage of industry evolution when buyers' needs and preferences are not yet clearly established, when search behavior on both sides of the market proceeds by trial and error, and when no single technical advance is likely to crystallize a new dominant design. As a result, although the technical ferment may be considerable, it is not always easy to see what it means for the terms of industry competition.

The development of the transistor industry during the 1950s provides a richly documented instance of the architectural phase of innovation. Beginning in 1951 with the first commercial production of a transistor by Western Electric, a number of firms (RCA, GE, Philco, and Texas Instruments among others) turned their attention to the development of various types of transistors and the processes needed to manufacture them. These new products did, it is true, compete with vacuum tubes for some established applications, but their overall effect was to create whole new markets. In 1954, for example, Texas Instruments introduced the silicon junction transistor, which so greatly increased the temperature range within which the product could operate that it opened up a vast arena of military applications.[1]

As this historical sketch suggests, innovation during the early years of product evolution is often closely linked to developments in science and research; yet although scientific breakthroughs can and do play an important role in fostering architectural innovation, the real driving force lies more commonly in the fresh packaging of existing ideas and research to meet new or previously unarticulated market needs. In competitive terms, the genius at this stage of innovation is manifest not so much in prize-winning scientific discoveries as in commercial perception—that is, in seeing and understanding the business-relevant links between existing technologies and untapped markets.

Once the basic architecture of a product has been established and its market linkages have begun to crystallize, innovation shifts into what we call its "regular" phase, which occupies the lower left-hand quadrant of figure 9.1. Technical changes of the regular sort tend to refine and extend established designs in both product and process and to strengthen established market linkages. These incremental innovations are, of course, much less dramatic than their architectural counterparts, but their cumulative impact may be every bit as substantial.[2]

Consider, for example, the homely but typical case of the electric light bulb:

By 1909 the initial tungsten filament and vacuum bulb innovations were in place; from then until 1955 there came a series of incremental changes—better metal alloys for the filament[,] . . . coiling the filament, "frosting" the glass, and many more. In the same period the price of a 60 watt bulb decreased . . . from $1.60 to 20 cents each, the lumens output increased by 175 percent, the direct labor content was reduced . . . from 3 to 0.18 minutes per bulb . . .[3]

Between 1909 and 1955, therefore, the manufacture of electric light bulbs underwent gradual, measured, and incremental change in both product and process.

Advances of this sort are inevitably accompanied by process standardization and specialization, the progressive embodiment of human skills in machines, substantial changes in the nature of work, and the increasing rigidity of the whole production system. In one sense, of course, regular phase activity may spell competitive vulnerability, for competence that is embodied in capital equipment can be easily transferred. It may also, however, yield an enhanced ability to offer greater product variety—an ability that we think of as "market niche versatility."

In the early stages of regular phase development, variations in product performance often require major adjustments in product or process design. As the work of refinement proceeds, however, the range of performance available from a given design tends to increase, and this permits a firm to cover a broader set of market segments from the same or even a narrower technical base. In the post–World War II application of piston engines to commercial aircraft, to cite one example, the same manufacturing resources—tooling, equipment, and so forth—satisfied the requirements of small planes like the DC-3 and large planes like the DC-6 and Lockheed Constellation. Such versatility was simply not possible during the prewar days of industry evolution.

Even where such versatility does evolve, however, regular phase innovation enhances adaptation only to expected market demands. It does not—and cannot—prepare production systems for changes that are intrusive and unexpected. Much like the adaptation of a biological species to a given environmental niche, successful technical advances during the regular phase promote a varied and robust accommodation to the full range of familiar competitive circumstances. But, remember, even this heightened variety masks a deeper specialization that is vulnerable to sudden changes in the established terms of competition.

This vulnerability notwithstanding, incremental innovation is not limited to process/product refinements or to extensions of versatility in serving current markets. It may, in addition, add to the longevity of design concepts by creating new markets or market segments for the same products. The regular phase of innovation, then, does not affect extant market linkages; the "niche creation" phase, however, does. Falling in the upper left-hand quadrant of figure 9.1, it witnesses the re-packaging of established technology in support of efforts to reach new markets.

Of importance here are neither technical nor manufacturing challenges. Both are well understood. What matters is the fine-tuning of production systems to offer entrenched design concepts to new users. Consider, for example, the development of small chain saws when, in the mid-1970s, an energy crisis and a back-to-nature movement created a new market segment—the casual user—eager for lightweight, low-cost saws. Manufacturing these saws did require some incremental adjustments in product design and in process. Major changes, however, took place elsewhere: in target markets, in channels of distribution, in advertising, and in careful reading of individual consumer preferences about fashion and styling.[4]

No producer of chain saws was able to build a lasting advantage in the low-cost segment of the market because competitors were easily able to copy and extend the design concepts and manufacturing technology on which the new saws rested. This, too, is characteristic of the niche creation phase. Technical configurations geared to new market segments can be readily duplicated and, as a result, offer uncertain ground for building a sustainable competitive advantage. If, as the inelegant saying goes, anyone can buy the same cookie cutter that you use, it is no simple matter to build a great and lasting business on a distinctively shaped cookie.

The time comes, inevitably, when both regular and niche creation innovations are not enough to support a more permanent competitive vitality, for neither is intended to break out of the existing dominant design or even to challenge core concepts. Especially in mature industries, such innovations might help keep a company in business, but only to a rather limited point. When new technology develops or preferences change, firms will lose competitive position unless they are willing and able to apply substantially new design concepts to their established markets. This is not at all the same as what happens during the architectural phase of innovation, when epochal changes are used to create or define new markets. Applying new technology to existing markets is, rather, the essential feature of what we think of as the "revolutionary" phase of innovation (the lower right-hand quadrant of figure 9.1). When,

113

in the mid-1960s, IBM introduced its powerful S/360 computer system, the design concepts on which the system rested were not mere refinements of concepts embodied in previous machines. Nor were they, for the most part, dependent on technically novel components. True, the 360 did represent IBM's determination to move away from transistors and toward advanced integrated circuitry; nonetheless, its revolutionary nature lay in IBM's massive effort to create a single, software-compatible family of processors sharing common logic, components, and peripheral equipment. Moreover, this one system was intended to serve the same wide range of market applications then addressed by IBM's existing machines (the 1400 series, which was aimed at the data-processing needs of small- and medium-sized business, and the 7000 series, which was aimed at government agencies and larger corporations).

This notion of a common logic serving the whole market was a revolutionary departure from established practice at the level of overall product concept, and it demanded of IBM a $5 billion investment in software development and new manufacturing facilities. The 360 did not, of course, make obsolete all the skills and resources that IBM then possessed, but it certainly did upset established design hierarchies and fundamentally alter the terms of industry competition. By any reasonable measure, its transilience was extraordinary.[5]

III

In terms of the transilience matrix presented in figure 9.1, the process of industrial de-maturity, which depends on a shift from conservative to disruptive technical change, generally takes the form of a movement from the lower left- to the lower right-hand quadrant—that is, from the regular to the revolutionary phase of innovation. For our analysis of the American automobile industry, we have, therefore, a rather simple question to ask: did such a shift actually take place? In chapter 8 we presented market-related evidence to support our contention that de-maturity might be and, indeed, is happening. Here we want to know if the data on innovation corroborate or contradict that finding. If a careful look at the recent history of Detroit reveals in process the kind of developments our model of de-maturity would predict, then the model gains legitimacy as an explanation of industry evolution. Market behavior, as we noted, squares with our expectations. What about innovation?

To determine whether the dominant pattern of innovation has shifted, we must first have a detailed account of technological changes over time and an assessment of their impact on established systems of production. Accordingly,

we have compiled an extensive list of specific innovations in automobile technology in the United States between 1893 and 1981. This list—divided into
the four clusters of drive train, body and chassis, other product, and process
innovations—is presented in appendix D. Figure 9.2 provides a summary of
this data by presenting information about innovation in drive trains. Both the
appendix and figure 9.2 graph the effects of innovation on production systems
by assigning low values for transilience to conservative changes and high values to disruptive changes.

As these findings make clear, a period of significant architectural advance
in the early years of the century gave way to an era of gradual, regular phase
refinement during the heydey of the Model T and, then, to a spurt of revolutionary change with the introduction of the closed steel body in the mid-1920s.
Numerous improvements in suspension systems, engine design, and overall
ease and comfort of operation joined with the appearance of closed steel bodies
to create the famous "rolling living rooms" of the 1930s. With the addition
of automatic transmissions in the 1940s, the dominant design was completed
that was to hold the American market in its grip for the next thirty years.

From the late 1930s to the late 1950s, changes in this all-purpose roadcruiser
were largely a matter of incremental refinement and a growing emphasis on
niche creation. The V-8 engine, to take one example, was by no means new
to the industry, but several design changes during the late 1940s and early
1950s (in pistons, connecting rods, overhead valves, camshafts, and the like)
greatly boosted its horsepower-to-weight ratio. These refinements had little
impact on capital equipment or engineering skills, yet they gave eager market-
ers a high-compression engine with which to create the horsepower-oriented

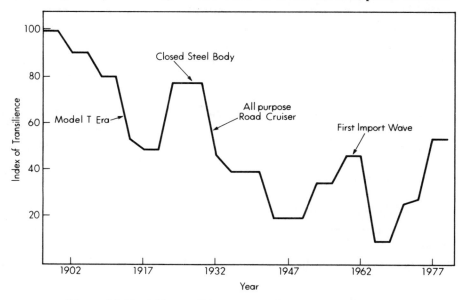

Figure 9.2 *Transilience of Innovation in Drive-Trains 1884–1980*

competition of the 1950s and 1960s. To define and serve a market niche concerned with speed, power, and rapid acceleration, V-8-powered "muscle cars" were essential. The technology of these muscle cars, however, could be—and was—easily imitated. Like most niche-creating innovations, these technical accomplishments did not supply the basis for a long-term competitive advantage.

With the first wave of imports in the late 1950s, the pattern of innovative activity began to change, and domestic producers turned their attention to building small cars. New engine concepts appeared in the market (most notably, the rear-mounted, air-cooled aluminum engine of the Corvair), and there were a host of changes in transmissions and in chassis design. That these developments represented a genuine movement away from the core concepts of the V-8 roadcruiser is evidenced by the rise in the transilience of technology during these years. When the import wave tailed off, so did the level of transilience. But this downward curve was only temporary. Growing regulatory pressures and changing market demands once more began to pry innovative activity away from the dominant design.

By the 1970s the shift in the character of innovation had clearly begun to accelerate. As before, changes did not first appear in core concepts but on the fringes of the design hierarchy. Producers initially directed their efforts toward simple reductions in the size of their cars; but as incentives for change persisted, they started to look beyond mere downsizing to front-wheel drive, transaxles, transverse-mounted engines, electronics, new materials, and new processes. As the scope of this innovative activity gradually spread up through the design hierarchy its implications for production systems began to come into focus. New tooling was needed, new performance specifications, new engineering tolerances, new component designs—in short, new skills on the part of both workers and managers. An industry once geared to minor technical advances and the peaceful rhythms of the annual model change gradually realized that the kind of change now demanded of it was of a much more fundamental sort.

Technical ferment during the mid to late 1970s calls itself to our attention, therefore, not for its novelty but for its impact on established modes of doing business. Still, the temptation remains to deny the nature of the unfamiliar challenge that has been taking shape. This, too, shall pass, diehards mutter, as the world they used to know irrevocably slips away. That it is slipping away and that a new one is coming into being are not the conclusions of idle speculation. The cumulative data on patterns of innovation, as on patterns of market response to technology, are hard to ignore. We have entered a phase of revolutionary change.

A further indication that such a phase has begun is the emergence not of isolated, but of clustered innovations—like those, for example, associated with the introduction of front-wheel drive. This clustering of technical effort is, as a rule, characteristic of a period of active market search, a period during which learning behavior and experimentation work their way, step by step, through a hierarchy of design concepts. In general, the closer the process gets to established core concepts, the greater the effect of each individual advance on all other design parameters. And if, as chapter 8 indicates, the market continues to place a premium on technology and, especially, on the diversity of technology, the more this interrelated search activity represents not a once-and-for-all adjustment in design concepts but an on-going process of de-maturity.

In the automobile industry, certainly, this process is far from being complete. To the contrary, all the available evidence suggests that open-ended search and learning are continuing on both sides of the market. Although the ultimate direction of this activity is unknowable, it is possible to infer from the thrust of current work at least some of the directions innovation will take in the years ahead. (We offer a brief summary of these directions in appendix D.)

Our analysis suggests that the course of innovation will proceed in two distinct stages, the first of which will involve advances in materials, electronics, and mechanical structures that improve the efficiency and performance of existing engines and power trains. Many of these developments will naturally appear in clusters, such as the innovative cluster essential to perfecting advanced diesels. Improved methods of fuel delivery, turbocharging, and high temperature operation will require, for example, advances in electronic control systems as well as in heat-resistant materials, like ceramics. Other developments—of a plastic engine, say—would have even farther-reaching effects. Sixty percent lighter and thirty percent quieter than any metal counterpart, it would revolutionize the economics of engine production by reducing machining needs, energy requirements, and scrap levels.[6]

Stage I innovations (post-1983) may well include significant changes in processes, too. Recent work promises benefits from, among much else, a casting process in which styrofoam is used to make parts molds.[7] By eliminating traditional constraints in the fabrication of molds, this "lost foam" approach might so reduce the complexity of the task that costs would be dramatically lowered. At the extreme, the use of lost foam might even make possible a disposable engine—that is, an engine so inexpensive to build that it would be cheaper to replace than repair.

A second stage of innovations will go beyond changes of this sort to core concepts themselves. If the incentives for innovation persist, for example, the whole fuel and energy conversion logic of the automobile may change.[8] Gasoline and diesel-based combustion systems have dominated the industry for the better part of the century, but enhanced battery technology and better mastery of chemical processes could make an electric-powered car feasible. Nor are more radical changes—a turbine engine powered by hydrogen, for example—out of the question. It takes no great leap of the imagination to see the truly revolutionary effect such a shift in core concepts would have on all aspects of manufacturing and market linkage. Once set in motion, so fundamental an upheaval in long-established design hierarchies would keep the ferment of de-maturity alive to the end of the century and beyond.

The point worth noting here is not that one or another advance is somehow definitely in the cards but that the possibilities being explored are sufficiently revolutionary in their nature and transilient in their potential effect on markets and production systems that the process of de-maturity may well continue for some time. Thus here, as in many other manufacturing industries, a—or perhaps the—key problem for the 1980s and beyond will remain how to manage under conditions of increasing technical ferment, for these conditions are not apt soon to disappear.

Chapter 10

The Renaissance
of American
Manufacturing

AS Washington Irving imagined him, Rip Van Winkle slept through the American Revolution. When he dozed off after a hard day of squirrel hunting and an even harder bout of drinking in the mountains above the Hudson River, George III sat upon the throne of England. When he awoke, an entirely different George was president of the newly independent United States. The latter-day Rip, whom we imagined stirring to life at the beginning of this book, would have passed in gentle slumber events no less momentous. While he slept, a stable, long-established empire of commerce has broken apart, and the rules and precedents that bound it together now prove a poor guide to the vigorous but unfamiliar competition that has sprung up in its place.

Considered in this light, the central challenge today is to master both the work of production and the competitively significant development of process/product technology. This is the task. But on what inherited resources can we call? Were the challenge merely to reduce costs by a certain percentage or to prune inventories to a certain level, we would have a good sense of the tools to bring to the job. But when, as in the automobile industry, it is to reach such goals by building and guiding an organization that is altogether responsive to an on-going process of learning—about markets, about technology, about production systems, and about the linkages among them—the tools are not so obvious, the inherited resources not so apparent.

A bit like the early explorers and mapmakers, whose general task it was to push back the frontier by discovering and charting previously unknown territory, today's managers cannot know in advance precisely what they will find in the region out beyond the most recent dominant design. Unlike those earlier explorers, however, managers do not really have the luxury of refusing to set out on the journey. Competitive pressures force them to undertake the expedition; deciding not to go virtually guarantees the ultimate erosion or collapse of the ground on which they currently stand. All they can do is to be prepared for anything, ready to see everything, determined to ignore nothing—because only after they discover what the terrain is like will they discover exactly what it is they are called upon to do. More than ever before, to manage will be to learn.

II

For those managers charged with the oversight of technology—that is, with both developing the technical resources of their companies and bringing them to bear on market opportunities—the art of frontier survival does not depend on waiting patiently for a miraculous breakthrough in the laboratory. Between initial explorations of a new technology, xerography for example, and its embodiment in commercially desirable products lies a painstaking sequence of supporting innovations, refinements, and modifications. These do not just happen of themselves; they must be actively managed. Moreover, as the life cycles of successful products unfold, the emphasis of that managerial work will itself evolve. The skills needed to map out an entirely new area are not the same as those needed to prepare it for permanent settlement.

During the architectural phase of innovation, for example, lack of certainty about user preferences as well as about the full extent of a technology's possibilities makes regular informal communication—among researchers, between researchers and specialists in other functions, and between researchers and users—of central importance. Lack of certainty also places a premium on the enlistment of individuals who do not need all details spelled out in advance, who respond well to ambiguous or ill-defined tasks, who are open to new ideas, and whose particular expertise does not blind them to the opportunities that might pop up in unexpected places. To support the open-ended efforts of which such people are capable, sponsoring organizations must provide an incentive system that rewards, not penalizes, the taking of risks. Some experts would argue that this is the way technology should be managed all the time. Our point is simply that, during the architectural phase, this is the way it must be managed.

Once core concepts have been established, however, and innovation moves into the regular phase, the work of technology management undergoes a corresponding change. As user preferences and technical limits become better known, objectives become clearer and are more efficiently served by sharply focused specialists. By the same token, there is less of a premium on informal communication and the more extreme forms of risk-taking. Keeping on top of developments in the technology is still essential, but the frame of reference is different. The task at hand is to push an existing design forward, to make incremental adjustments, to locate missing pieces of the puzzle. Earlier efforts provided a general outline map; the challenge now is to fill in the details.

These shifts in managerial emphasis reflect the increased costs of change as products and processes evolve. During the architectural phase, few organizational barriers restrict the flow of research and development into still flexible manufacturing operations; during the regular phase, by contrast, there are often endless forms to file, capital budgets to meet, signatures to obtain, and committees to persuade. The emerging logic of production economies mandates close monitoring and regulation of anything that might disrupt increasingly standardized operations, and this "buffering" of manufacturing tends rapidly to become not merely a by-product of growth but an explicit managerial goal. It promotes efficiency and allows for incremental change, but it does so by creating barriers that did not exist before. If well managed, it can serve competitively valuable ends; if poorly managed, however, if carried too far or employed too reflexively, it can undermine competitive ability.

Consider, for example, the case of Ampex, an early leader in the production of video broadcast recorders.[1] At first, design engineers and manufacturing people were located in the same facility, shared comparable goals, and kept in close touch. As volume grew and as the need to lower costs grew with it, manufacturing not only physically moved away from the development center; its objectives and priorities changed as well. To maintain the smooth transfer of products from development to production, the company tried a number of organizational expedients (pilot plants, new product groups, and so on), but in a company as engineering-driven as Ampex no such after-the-fact device could circumvent the barriers of distance and altered priorities. Cut off from immediate daily contact with production, engineering became so involved with the ramifications of product technology that it lost touch with the manufacturing process.

Failed communication—whether because the lines of communication are too long, too fuzzy, or too slow or because, left to themselves, organizational units tend to develop their own agendas—can spell disaster in the marketplace. Consider, for instance, the following account from the history of the American radio industry:

> One of the earliest designs for an all-transistor miniature portable radio was developed in the mid-fifties in the corporate lab of one of the giant American companies. The link to the company's own radio business was never forged, although the circuit was licensed to a Japanese producer who incorporated it into products sold successfully in the U.S. Later, the American firm's radio business, attempting to catch up, made a photocopy of the Japanese circuit board as the basis for their own design, only to learn to everyone's chagrin that they were copying an invention of their own lab.[2]

Barriers and buffers, whatever their form, do not inevitably lead to trouble. The more stable an industry's technology and the more mature its competitive structure, the more individual firms can let incremental refinements of products and processes move ahead in separate (and non-communicating) organizational units—subject, of course, to formalized controls imposed from above. And top managers, who in a stable setting more and more lose touch with the technological base of their companies, are only too glad to rely on such formalized controls. A rationalized production system, after all, demands carefully defined targets, precise planning, elaborate schedules, and orderly improvements. Predictability is the key. True, no industry is so utterly stable that predictability can be guaranteed or communications linkages between design and manufacturing eliminated altogether. But the drift toward maturity tends to emphasize the value, not the danger, of buffering operations.

Under conditions of de-maturity, however, organizational arrangements well suited to the gradual refinement of old designs will prove a great competitive liability. Reaction to changes in technology or the market will be slow; lead times will stretch out; the transfer of new ideas into production processes will happen only with difficulty. As a result, the informal communication, risk-taking behavior, and openness to learning that characterized operations during the architectural phase of innovation once again become essential, but there can be no literal return to the free-form structures of that earlier period. Managers cannot now start, as they once did, from scratch. A complex organization is already in place, and it cannot be wished away. The challenge, of course, is to start with these entrenched structures and make them responsive to the new terms—and pace—of competition.

Managing innovation in a de-maturing industry is not the same, then, as managing in a young industry enjoying its first full spurt of growth. Like the manufacturers of propeller aircraft—Boeing, for example—that successfully made the switch to jets, producers facing de-maturity will also face substantial constraints on their operating costs, allowable parameters of product performance and reliability, and freedom to reshape customer expectations. Their markets will not be tiny or inchoate or lacking in a strong sense of what an acceptable product must do or cost. Their industry will have had a long enough history to establish well-defined expectations in customers' minds. If Boeing's work on jet aircraft had resulted in a product that was twice as fast but only one-tenth as reliable as the older propeller planes, no commercial airline would have beaten a path to its door.[3]

De-maturity throws open design concepts and production processes that have grown relatively closed to anything but minor change, but it does not follow that every old idea or approach or technique will be discarded. Much that is familiar will go, but much will remain to frame the context for that which is new. Potential users might not know in function or price what to ask of a nuclear-powered toothbrush, but they do know what to ask of a new aircraft design. Or, for that matter, of a design for a diesel locomotive. Long prior experience with steam-driven engines placed explicit limits on the basic configuration of an acceptable product, limits that the diesel—for all its performance advantages—had to observe if it were to be not only a technical but also a commercial success.

During an earlier phase of industry evolution, managers could try out new design concepts in very short production runs, sell them to a small group of customers, listen to the reactions, tinker as needed with products or processes, and only then scale up operations. Here, managers confront the necessity of innovating in the context of well-established markets, high production volumes, and pointed expectations about product costs, reliability, and performance. There is, in short, no commercial moratorium during de-maturity, no relaxed breathing space for managers to rethink their course. There is, instead, the competitive necessity of making relatively major changes in products and processes without seriously interrupting the flow of goods to the market. It is as if during a performance of *Hamlet*, the actors had to rehearse on stage a production of *Rosencrantz and Guildenstern Are Dead*—and to rehearse it without the audience noticing or feeling that it had been cheated or asking for its money back at the box office. Even the Bard himself allowed time for changes of scene.

III

Although the burden that both heightened technical ferment and enhanced competition place on the management of production systems is immense, it is not unprecedented. Looking at that which already exists and trying to envision something quite different is never easy, but surely that was the managerial challenge that Henry Ford confronted during the early days of the automobile industry. Surely that was the challenge the nation confronted in adapting its industrial base to military production during World War II. Our task today is of comparable magnitude. The details may be different: to incorporate particular new technologies and heightened product variety into high-volume manufacturing systems and to do so without the luxury of long lead times. But the essential challenge is the same: to draw from past experience and present imagination the will, vision, and expertise to meet future needs.

Merely relying on new product technologies like ceramics or putting such new process equipment as robots on the factory floor will not, however, suffice. Complementary changes in what we spoke of in chapter 1 as the "software" of management are every bit as important. The skillful implementation of technology matters as much as does the quality of technical design. If managers continue to view a production system as a limited, neutral piece of apparatus, which is to be blindly run according to fixed design specifications and used by rote to meet budgeted cost objectives and volume levels, they will enjoy no greater benefit from the new technology than if they had mistaken it for a coat rack. What is needed is a view of production as an enterprise of unlimited potential, an enterprise in which current arrangements are but the starting point for continuous organizational learning. No omniscient engineer ever handed down a design for product or production that could not stand improvement, that was perfectly suited to all possible changes in market preference or technical capability. And there is no point in trying to manage production as if such an engineer or such a design did exist.

We do not mean, of course, that learning should proceed while schedules and shipping deadlines get ignored; competent management requires simultaneous attention to both current tasks and future possibilities. But given their ingrained habit of attention to problems of the moment, production managers are far more likely to sacrifice the uncertain rewards of the latter for the assured returns of the former. What gets lost in the shuffle is the intimate connection between the two.

Nothing, for example, can so improve bottom-line results in today's marketplace as a substantial increase in product quality, yet final quality is altogether dependent on what happens in design, in engineering, in manufacturing, in maintenance, in supervision, in marketing, in the work of assemblers, in the operations of suppliers, and so on. When communication among and within these groups is lacking, when top management loses touch with their efforts, when organizational barriers or procedures or suspicions divide them, the timely flow of information and the integration of effort essential to market success do not take place. Or do not take place as well as they might. Not only is learning sacrificed; so, too, are market results.

Building a truly competitive organization also requires active enlistment of the best efforts of workers, especially line workers. Their skills, commitment, and enthusiasm are the means by which strategic goals get translated into practice; equally important, though less often acknowledged, their experience in the day-to-day work of production is the means by which an organization learns—if it learns. To give workers inadequate training in the technologies with which they must deal, to treat them as mindless drones suitable only for dull, repetitive tasks, or to ignore the vast contribution they can make when integrated into a coherent manufacturing system is to throw away through sheer carelessness or, worse, unthinking prejudice a uniquely valuable corporate resource. There may have been a time when a sweatshop mentality, whatever its social noxiousness, proved useful in the market. That time has long since disappeared.

Thus, only when grafted onto a production system dedicated to on-going learning and communication, only when used in tandem with a skilled and responsible work force, can new technologies realize their potential as competitive weapons. Only when such a work force is truly engaged in the enterprise and encouraged to learn and excel, can a company hope to introduce competitively successful new products in a timely fashion. Innovation is no substitute for competent work-force management or for a mastery of production. The future does not belong to firms that try to make up for poor work-force management or sloppy plants with cutting-edge technology. Nor does it belong to firms that do not bother with new advances in technology because their factories are well run by present standards. The future belongs only to those firms—and managers—who eagerly seize opportunities on both fronts. Doing well in the new industrial competition calls for more than a piecemeal effort; it requires the deliberate application to market opportunities of technical competence harnessed to all the strengths of a production system. Nothing less will do.

IV

There is much good sense in the reflective judgment of one historian that the Renaissance was

in a peculiar way, an age of transition. Every age is, of course, more or less transitional, since it is in the nature of history to be constantly changing. The fleeting present is ever the transitional link through which all our yesterdays flow uninterruptedly into the infinite succession of tomorrow and tomorrow and tomorrow. But there are few periods in the history of western civilization—I would venture to say not more than two, unless our own age should prove to be a third—in which the transition from the preceding to the following age makes so complete a transformation that it may be regarded as a change in kind rather than in degree. Such a change was involved in the transition from medieval to modern civilization. And the Renaissance owes much of its peculiar character, I think, to the uneasy coexistence within it of medieval and modern elements, of decaying or obsolescent institutions and ways of thinking, together with new institutions and ideas still imperfectly formed.[4]

True enough, but there was more to the Renaissance than that. The ideas and institutions in the process of emergence had—or were felt to have—close ties not to the era immediately preceding but to the experience of classical antiquity. What came to flower in the Renaissance was an extraordinary communal effort to repossess, reinterpret, and extend the significant achievements of a deeply valued cultural past.

Meeting the challenge of the new industrial competition requires of American manufacturers much the same kind of effort, an effort that is indeed underway. In numerous plants and factories throughout the country, remarkable things are now going on. To be sure, these revitalized operations do not yet represent a majority of the nation's productive activity or even a majority of the activity in those industries directly threatened by de-maturity. But the signs of this industrial renaissance are already well enough established and its accomplishments have already reached a sufficient critical mass for us to speak of them as parts of a broad-based process of renewal.

Our visits to the factories of U.S. automobile firms where this renewal, this commitment to competitive excellence, is in full swing, uncovered a spirit and a level of performance every bit as impressive as that which we found in Japan. In an older engine plant, for example, we encountered a crew of line workers responsible for building water pumps who, a year previously, had been given encouragement as well as authority by the plant manager to improve their operations. Putting their heads together, they modified the layout of equipment, altered job assignments, changed material flows, sought out staff groups for technical support, and tinkered with process machinery—much of this on their own time. When we spoke with them, they had already become three times more productive than they had been before, had improved the quality of their pumps, and had reduced the amount of scrap from their operations by a factor of ten. This is not an isolated case. At an automobile assembly plant that we visited, rejection rates on the fit of front-end sheet metal (hoods, bumpers, and the like) averaged one out of every sixty vehicles. Changing a process involving more than fifty-four separate work stations is no easy matter; yet, when given the chance to restructure operations, workers lowered rejection rates within an eight month period from 1 in 60 to 1 in 18,000.

Treating the work force as a competitive asset is, of course, only one aspect of the best current efforts to institutionalize a new paradigm for production. "In the old days," a veteran plant manager told us,

the designs we had to build were pretty shlocky; they didn't fit together very well. But the guys on the line were pretty inventive, and they would usually figure out a way to make the design work. Now we've got ourselves a beautiful design; and with the approach we've got going with our people and with their involvement in making sure the product is right, we are turning out a superior product.

Advances in product and process design, a conscious effort to tear down the barriers that have grown up between manufacturing and the other functions, a deliberate effort to encourage on-going communication at all levels, and a willingness to learn from experience and to follow the possibilities of new technology—these are the minimum requirements for building a new manufacturing paradigm.

We have seen it take shape in GE's locomotive plant in Erie, Pennsylvania, where advanced automation has been combined with a new openness in communication and involvement of the work force. We have seen it in Cummins Engine's innovations in work-force management and product design, in Signetics' commitment to "never-ending improvement" in the quality of its semiconductors, in John Deere's application of the very latest manufacturing technologies, in Caterpillar's push toward low-cost manufacturing worldwide, in Timken's emphasis on product design and the maintenance of close relationships with users—in short, we have seen it take shape in dozens of companies, never in quite the same form but always directed toward the same end: building organizations that are absolutely first-rate in the work of technology-based manufacturing.

Although encouraging, these signs of an industrial renaissance are still limited; the developments they represent, still fragile. Lack of persistent support by—or a major change in skills and orientation among—top management, inability at middle levels to transcend the old certainties and the older prejudices, lukewarm or fickle commitment to the painful adjustments the new paradigm will require—any of these can stop the renaissance in its tracks, turn back the clock, and doom American industry to a new dark age of failed competitiveness in both domestic and international markets.

If, for any of these reasons, the renaissance now beginning should prove stillborn, our industrial fate will be no less ironic than tragic. For if the history of our manufacturing experience teaches us anything, it is that the key tasks

127

each generation faces in mastering the work of production are not identical with those of the generation before. In an important sense, of course, such mastery is cumulative. As the old iron mill at Saugus, Massachusetts, reminds us, no matter how great the outward differences in scale or complexity, the structure of some operations varies precious little over time. Still, the set of competitive issues that determine industrial success or failure do shift from one historical era to another and do call for different kinds of managerial energy and expertise.

It has long since become a familiar observation that generals regularly spend their time preparing to fight the previous war. Managers often do the same. Whether from the force of habit or from the appeal of comfortable modes of thought and action, they often fail to see how the problems that beset them are unlike those with which they have become familiar. Or they fail to make the painful effort to determine what from the past continues to apply, what does not, and what that is new must be learned. Yet this joint act of judgment and commitment is essential if the threat of late twentieth-century competition is to be translated into a genuine opportunity for industry renewal—to allow for the coming to fruition of "new institutions and ideas still imperfectly formed."

Appendices

Appendix A

Concentration and
Industry Evolution

CHANGE in the degree of an industry's concentration—that is, the number, size, and relative strength of competitors—plays a central role in defining the arena in which firms compete. The ideas developed in Chapter 2 provide a useful frame of reference for analyzing changes in concentration because it turns out that the concentration of an industry is neither fixed nor randomly changeable, but evolves in a predictable fashion as the industry itself evolves.

When a product is new and the industry devoted to it is just beginning to form, competitive structure is chaotic and fragmented. Because learning and experimentation proceed rapidly on both sides of the market, because production processes are still flexible and not very capital-intensive, and because entry and exit are fairly easy to accomplish, there may be a large number of competitors whose positions relative to each other are in constant flux. But as uncertainties decrease and as a dominant design emerges, the requirements of process innovation push the development of specialized, dedicated equipment and the achievement of production volume. No longer can the lone widget-maker rely on a few hand tools and a spare garage. To continue as a viable competitor, he must invest in relatively capital-intensive assets. This development inevitably flushes some small operations out of the industry and pushes others to the periphery, all of which reduces industry fragmentation and boosts concentration.[1]

But there are other forces tending toward concentration as well. The establishment of a dominant technical design is never simple or easy, for the inherent

131

"lumpiness" of new process technologies makes them difficult for an organization to digest. New equipment, which often requires large capital outlays, must be procured and mastered; new skills must be developed by workers and managers alike; new modes of control and communication must be devised and implemented. Because the new technology offers substantial reductions in the variable costs of production, the expense of accommodating it can often be justified only by greatly increasing production volumes. Hence, even though the emergence of a dominant design tends to be associated with overall market growth and the appearance of new customers, it is also associated with higher levels of industry concentration. A certain number of firms in an industry will be able to digest the lumpiness of new technology and, as a result, will enjoy a competitive advantage that draws customers away from other producers. The industry will be populated by fewer firms commanding larger shares of the market than was true before the dominant design crystallized.

Industry evolution does not, however, always result in higher levels of concentration. As product technology becomes more clearly defined and as the rate of process innovation diminishes, continued market growth creates opportunities for new entrants or peripheral firms to offer an increasing variety of products at or below the cost of the old product mix. The reason is simple. Once both product and process technologies are well understood and easily procurable (that is, once they are embodied in capital equipment that can be readily purchased, in designs that can be readily copied, or in human skills that can be readily hired), nonestablished firms—including foreign importers—will usually take the lead in identifying and exploiting new market niches. Unless there are substantial barriers to entry, overall market growth will outdistance growth in the market shares of leading competitors. In short, as industry development puts a premium on economies of scale in production and on the stability of capital-intensive technology, the very appropriability of that technology works to make the industry less concentrated.

In general, then, the development of industry structure depends on the interplay between market growth and technological innovation. If growth in the market plus technical stability leads to industry deconcentration, a slowing of growth or a major upheaval in production technology will likely produce a market contested by fewer—and larger—competitors. We do not mean that the absolute number of competitors will necessarily fall, although that may happen. We mean only that the rate of deconcentration will slow down. Faced with the need to digest lumpy new technologies, larger firms tend to get larger, and smaller firms tend to exit an industry, merge, or suffer a relative loss of position.

We are suggesting, therefore, that industry evolution is best understood as

132

a process of ebb and flow in the number, size, and strength of competitors—a process, we must emphasize, that depends on the frequency and magnitude of changes in production technology and on the overall rate of market growth. If major technical changes are relatively infrequent and if growth—even slow growth—persists over a long period of time, we would expect to see long-term deconcentration. If, however, growth slows and lumpy technological changes are common, we would expect to see a movement toward higher levels of concentration.

What happens, though, when dominant product designs—and not merely process technology—become open to change? The unlocking or unfreezing of the design hierarchy, as chapter 2 tried to show, is the prime engine of industry de-maturity, although its effects on industry structure are, at least in the first instance, much like those of process upheaval. As established links between market preference and technical configuration break down, the search for a new configuration will focus initially not on core concepts but on items well down the design hierarchy. Change usually comes first where the costs of change are least. Because movement up that hierarchy is inherently lumpy (it is increasingly capital-intensive and requires new organizational skills), changes below the level of core concepts tend to enhance the competitive position of firms with relatively large market shares—so long, of course, as these firms continue to adhere to the existing dominant design.

If, however, the process of market search comes to focus on core concepts themselves, the possibility exists for a technology-based new entry into the industry or for a substantial increase in the market share of small and/or peripheral firms. This is so because a shift in core concepts destroys the competence of established competitors at the same time that it allows other producers to gain market share by introducing new concepts. Market preference for new technical configurations removes the advantage enjoyed by industry leaders as a result of their past investments and places a premium on technical capabilities that they do not have. De-maturity works to undercut the benefits conferred by an entrenched position in the old technology, and so it leads, over time, toward industry deconcentration.

The internationalization of the automobile industry has wrought precisely the kind of change in industry structure that we might expect, following this line of argument. In figure A.1, which tracks developments among producers selling cars in the American market, we measure shifts in industry structure over time by calculating year by year the number of equivalent firms. Do not be misled by the apparently slight range of variation in the number of equivalent firms: a decline from four to three, for example, is tantamount to having a competitor with a fourth of the market drop out of the business entirely.

133

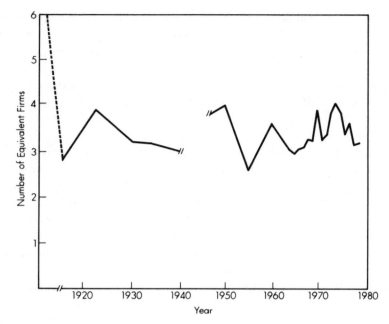

Figure A.1 *Trends in U.S. Automobile Market Structure*

SOURCE: 1900–1965: Abernathy, *Productivity Dilemma,* (1978), p. 30. 1966–1979: Calculated from data in *Ward's Automotive Yearbook,* (various years).

NOTE: The number of "equivalent firms" is calculated as defined in the text.

At several points in the industry's history between 1900 and 1955, adjustments of this magnitude have taken place: before World War I, when the introduction of the Model T and its associated production systems reduced the number of equivalent firms from eleven to three; between 1924 and 1926, with the introduction of closed steel bodies; and between 1948 and 1954, with the adoption of automated transfer lines. In each case, the application of capital-intensive process technology substantially boosted production economies of scale and, in turn, raised the level of industry concentration (as measured by a *decrease* in the number of equivalent firms).

Since 1955—not counting the GM strike in 1970—there have been two additional periods of concentration: in the early 1960s, with the introduction by domestic producers of compact cars made on new automated equipment; and during the mid-1970s, when those same producers undertook their "downsizing" programs in earnest. Throughout the industry's history, technical upheavals have had the effect, at least initially, of raising industry concentration. The overall trend, however, at least since World War II, has been toward an increase in the number of equivalent firms.

134

If periods of technical ferment have tended first to concentrate the domestic industry, growth in both market size and international trade—especially when combined with the increased appropriability of the new technology—have worked in the opposite direction. As figure 4.1 indicates, this opposite movement—toward deconcentration—has been quite dramatically in evidence in the automobile industry worldwide.

Appendix B

Comparative Analysis of Cost and Productivity

ANY COMPARISON of productivity and cost data for U.S. and Japanese auto makers must confront a number of thorny problems—among them, different reporting practices, different levels of vertical integration, and different product mix. In each case we began with annual reports and other generally available financial statements, but we supplemented them with studies carried out by industry consultants, Wall Street analysts, government agencies, and academics. We also spoke at length with industry executives and union officials and, in some cases, were given access to proprietary studies carried out by the firms themselves or their suppliers. We then made a concerted effort to check our findings through detailed field research both in the United States and in Japan.

Notes to Table 5.1

Data on compensation rates are taken from: 1) "A Million Jobs to Go," *Forbes* (November 23, 1981), p. 40, which contains estimates compiled by GM; 2) "Wages and Working Conditions in the Japanese Automobile Industry," an unpublished 1981 study by the staff of the Japan Autoworkers Union; and 3) extensive conversations with industry and union officials and an examination of the provisions of collective bargaining agreements.

Notes to Table 5.2

Hours per vehicle

We established these figures by taking domestic employment as reported in 1979 annual reports and multiplying by average hours worked per person per year to get total hours worked. We then divided total hours worked by total domestic vehicle production. Doing this gave us "raw" hours per vehicle. Next, we adjusted for vertical integration. Since all producers had a ratio of value added to sales of about 0.4 (GM's was 0.54), we brought GM into line with other producers by adjusting its raw hours to a 40 percent vertical integration level (by multiplying its raw hours by .4/.54). This adjustment affects all factors of production in proportion to the ratio of new value added to old value added.

To correct for product mix, we used data on manufacturing costs by vehicle size developed in 1974 for the Committee on Motor Vehicle Emissions of the National Research Council and reported in Toder, *Trade Policy and the U.S. Automobile Industry* (New York: 1978), pp. 132–134. We were careful, however, to correct for changes in materials and labor since 1974. Then we used Ford's and GM's shares in the small, medium, and large car segments to estimate a weighted average of relative labor costs (with small cars taking a value of 1.00). The details are presented in table B.1. Dividing the hours per vehicle for the average product mix by the product mix factor just developed gave us the hours per vehicle for Ford (84) and GM (83) reported in table 5.2.

We determined the comparable figures for Toyo Kogyo and Nissan by increasing the raw hours per vehicle calculated from their annual reports by 15 percent. This adjustment was based on studies, which were conducted by an American manufacturer, of the in-house work content of similar parts. We made it in spite of the fact that Toyo Kogyo's and Nissan's ratio of value added to sales, as given in their annual reports, approximates the 40 percent level assumed in our analysis. If anything, therefore, we have probably overestimated the number of labor hours per vehicle for Japanese producers.

Purchased components and materials

We began with data in Ford's and GM's annual reports on purchases per vehicle, which we then adjusted for vertical integration (the effect being to raise GM's purchases by 30 percent and to lower Ford's by 5 percent). As with our calculation of labor hours, we corrected for product mix—here by using a scale

TABLE B.1

Product Mix Factor

	Small	Car Size Medium	Large
Production Shares			
Ford	0.11	0.68	0.21
GM	0.20	0.41	0.39
Relative Labor Cost per Vehicle	1.00	1.30	1.50
Weighted Average Relative Labor Cost			
Ford		1.31	
GM		1.32	

NOTE: The product mix factor for a given company is calculated by multiplying the relative labor cost per vehicle for each size class by the share of production in that size class and then summing across size classes. Thus, for Ford, the calculation is $(0.11 \times 1.00) + (0.68 \times 1.30) + (0.21 \times 1.50) = 1.31$. This number indicates that Ford's labor cost per vehicle is 1.31 times what it would be if Ford only made small cars.

of 1.00 for small cars, 1.35 for medium-sized cars, and 1.71 for large cars—and came up with a weighted average of 1.38 for Ford and 1.45 for GM. Since the figures with which we began were for 1979, we updated them to 1981 by increasing purchases per vehicle by 3 percent per year, a number that reflects both a rise in prices and an offsetting gain in productivity. The 3 percent figure, moreover, is taken from data on Nissan—so that we have, in effect, applied the Japanese experience to U.S. producers. (Note that these product mix adjustments tend to understate the cost difference between the United States and Japan.)

From these totals we have subtracted about $150 per car (or 2 to 3 percent of the sales price) as representing energy costs. This operation does not change the final cost figures but only their division between purchased components and other manufacturing costs.

For the Japanese producers, we could not rely on annual reports because purchases are not reported there. Hence, we turned instead to a study of Nissan conducted by Martin L. Anderson of M.I.T. ("Strategic Organization of the Japanese Automotive Groups," unpublished paper, April 1981). Anderson, in turn, employed the Japanese language version of Nissan's 1978 annual report to the Ministry of Finance (something like the American 10-K), compiled data on Nissan's suppliers, and corrected for differences in exchange rates (he used 212 yen per dollar; we use 220, the exchange rate for 1981). The result, $2858 per vehicle, we applied to both Nissan and Toyo Kogyo.

138

Other manufacturing costs

To capture the energy costs, depreciation, warranty costs, and the miscellaneous expenses included here, we relied on annual reports, studies by consultants and by U.S. producers, discussions with industry executives, and the work of Martin Anderson. The company studies gave us a starting point: estimates of total non-in-house labor manufacturing costs, from which we subtracted our estimates for materials and components before adjusting for differences in depreciation (GM is higher than Ford).

We derived comparable figures for the Japanese by using both Anderson's data on fixed costs at Nissan, which imply a difference between U.S. and Japanese producers of some $123 to $624 per car, and a report by James E. Harbour ("Comparison and Analysis of Manufacturing Productivity," final consultant report, Harbour and Associates, Dearborn Heights, Michigan, 1980), which contains information on warranty costs and depreciation. Together, these sources suggested that a Japanese advantage on the order of $300 to $400 was reasonable, a difference that reflects somewhat higher energy costs in Japan but much lower warranty and depreciation costs.

Nonmanufacturing costs

We estimated the costs of shipping, marketing, and distribution by looking first at annual report data on selling and general administrative expenses. Most Wall Street analysts and industry executives cite a figure of $400 for the costs added to a Japanese car by ocean freight and U.S. tariffs (see Abernathy, Harbour, and Henn, "Productivity and Comparative Cost Advantages," report to the U.S. Department of Transportation, 26 December 1980, pp. 56–58). U.S. producers have, on average, nonmanufacturing costs of $300–$350 per vehicle; the Japanese, $1100–$1200. The still higher number given for Nissan reflects the fact that Nissan reports greater selling and administrative expenses than any of the other Japanese auto makers.

Notes to Table 5.3

The data on labor hours per vehicle for different production processes were obtained from: James E. Harbour, "Comparison and Analysis of Manufacturing Productivity," final consultant report, Harbour and Associates, Dearborn Heights, Michigan, 1980. The data have been adjusted for differences in vertical integration.

Notes to Table 5.4

Our calculations of capital employed per vehicle are worked out in detail for Ford and Toyo Kogyo in table B.2, which takes into account the effects of inflation as well as differences in prices and currency values. We began with the annual reports for 1979, which provide data both on the gross book value of plant (including land) and equipment and on the value of work-in-process inventory. We translated the Toyo Kogyo figures into dollars in two ways: at a general exchange rate of 220 yen to the dollar and at a purchasing-power–parity exchange rate of 267 yen to the dollar. We applied purchasing-power–parity exchange rate estimates prepared by Irving Kravis et al., *International Comparisons of Real Product and Purchasing Power* (Baltimore: Johns Hopkins University Press, 1973), which we updated by using the appropriate deflators from the U.S. and Japanese national income accounts. The results for book value show Ford at $15.3 billion and Toyo Kogyo at either $1.54 billion or $1.27 billion, depending on the exchange rate used.

To adjust for inflation, we restated these book values in 1979 dollars, using rough estimates of the age of the capital stock and the business fixed-investment deflators from the national accounts. This gives us replacement values—that is, an approximation of what it would cost to replace the capital stock at today's prices. The formula for the adjustment factor can be written as:

$$k = P(1979) \, / \, P(1979 - \text{age})$$

where P is the investment deflator; the number in parentheses is the year in which the price is measured; and age is calculated as the ratio of accumulated depreciation to annual depreciation. Since the ages of the capital stock at Ford (8.1 years) and Toyo Kogyo (9.4 years) are comparable and since the rates of inflation are fairly close, these adjustments had little effect.

Then, after adding material and work-in-process inventory (which is not inflation adjusted) to gross plant and equipment, we present in section III of table B.2 our estimates of capital per vehicle. We also performed the same set of calculations for GM and Nissan, although—as previously—we corrected GM's data for differences in vertical integration. This probably overstated the

Comparative Analysis of Cost and Productivity

TABLE B.2

Capital Labor Ratios and Capital Productivity (1979)

Category	Ford	Toyo Kogyo General[1] Exchange Rate	Specific[2] Exchange Rate
I. Plant and Equipment (billions of dollars)			
Book Value	$15.330	$1.539	$1.269
Adjusted for Inflation[3]	26.975	2.509	2.068
II. Inventory[4] (materials and work in process– (billions of dollars)	$ 2.939	$0.077	$0.077
III. Capital per Vehicle[5] (dollars)			
Book Value	$3,048	$1,639	$1,351
Adjusted	5,052	2,623	2,161

SOURCES: Company annual reports for 1979. Deflators were taken from Ministry of Finance, Japan Monthly Finance Review no. 92 (December 1980); and Economic Report of the President; together with the Annual Report of the Council of Economic Advisers (Washington: U.S. Government Printing Office, 1981); and Organization for Economic Cooperation and Development, *Historical Statistics* (Paris, 1978). Purchasing power parity exchange rates were taken from Irving B. Kravis, et al., *International Comparisons of Real Product and Purchasing Power* (Baltimore: Johns Hopkins University Press, 1978).
NOTES: 1. Average 1979 exchange rate: 220 yen per dollar.
2. Capital formation exchange rate (structures and equipment) calculated based on data in Kravis et al., *International Comparisons of Real Product and Purchasing Power:* 267 yen per dollar in 1979—applies only to gross plant and equipment.
3. To correct plant and equipment for inflation, book values were restated in 1979 prices based on age of capital and variation in equipment and structures deflator from national income accounts; only estimated capital used in vehicle production is included (calculated based on fraction of total sales in automotive).
4. Inventory includes materials and work-in-process.
5. Vehicles include cars and trucks; excludes tractors for Ford.

amount of capital GM employed, for the operations it farmed out to vendors would likely have been less capital intensive than the GM average. But note, however, that the figures for Ford and GM pertain to both domestic and international operations. Since their European operations are less capital intensive than those in the United States, our overall capital estimates probably understate the Japanese advantage.

Appendix C

Technology and Market Demand

For the period 1961–1981, we took advertisements from fall issues of a widely read general interest magazine *(Time)*, compiled a list of the product characteristics mentioned most frequently, and—as table C.1 shows—divided those characteristics into four categories: technology, luxury/styling, performance, and economy. For each year we selected a total of forty-eight different ads, determined whether each characteristic mentioned in them was "stated" or only "implied," and then assigned a priority that reflected the characteristic's importance to the message of the ad. Something coded "primary stated," for example, might appear in a large headline or be the principal selling point; something coded "secondary stated" might be a point mentioned in the body of the text. Finally, we assigned a value of 3 points to characteristics of primary importance and 2 points to those of secondary importance. Average cumulative scores by category by year are presented in table C.2.

In order to identify trends in the data on technology and to eliminate statistical "noise," we have rounded and smoothed the data using methods described by John W. Tukey in *Exploratory Data Analysis* (Reading, Mass.: Addison-Wesley, 1977), pp. 205–230. The results are given in table C.2 under the heading "trend." To test our approach further, we experimented with a number of other weighting schemes, among them: using different advertising evaluators, applying other modes of scoring, and measuring the fraction of advertisements that was predominantly technological. We found that our results were insensitive to these adjustments.

TABLE C.1

Product Characteristics in the Advertising Analysis

Technology	Economy of Operation and Ownership
Engine Location	Price Given
Transverse Engine	Price Mentioned
OVH Cam	Resale Value
Front-Wheel Drive	Warranty
Rack-and-Pinion	Repair Cost
Disc Brakes	Rebates
Brakes in General	Actual MPG
Four-Cylinder Engine	Approximate MPG
Rotary Engine	Driving Range
Diesel Engine	Dealer Network
Special Engine Material	Durability
Fuel Injection	Quality-Craftsmanship
Technology General	Serviceability
Technology Specific	
Engineering Mentioned	

Performance	Styling and Luxury
Four-Wheel Drive	Options (nonperformance)
Handling	Styling
Automatic Transmission	Luxury
V-8 Engine	Interior Comfort
Acceleration (Power)	Interior Space
Smooth Ride	Quiet Ride
Suspension	
Safety	
Visibility	

Market Value of Technology

The purpose of these calculations was to test for a change in the market value of technology before and after the oil shock of 1979. Accordingly, we used data from 1977–1978, a period of falling real oil prices and a market shift toward larger cars, as a base point of reference. One possible complication—the nonexistence in this earlier period of technology available later—turned out on examination to be no complication at all. Although some of the technical efforts stimulated by the first oil shock in 1973–1974 had not yet worked their way into the market, most of the relevant technology (diesel engines, say, or front-wheel drive) had. In fact, some technical measures, like average driving range and package efficiency among compacts and subcompacts, were virtually identical in the two periods.

143

TABLE C.2

Index of Advertising Emphasis (1961–1981)

| | Domestic Cars | | | | | Imported Cars | | | | |
| | Technology | | Economy | Performance | Styling | Technology | | Economy | Performance | Styling |
	basic	trend				basic	trend			
1961	.857	.86	2.829	3.829	3.771	.860	.85	6.615	2.692	2.615
1962	.846	.85	3.000	3.333	4.718	1.111	1.11	4.667	1.778	2.111
1963	.925	.93	1.650	4.125	4.800	2.750	1.63	4.375	2.875	1.500
1964	.950	.93	1.125	3.950	5.300	1.625	2.75	3.250	2.000	2.250
1965	.889	.95	.528	4.222	4.056	4.333	3.85	3.000	3.500	2.667
1966	2.229	1.06	.914	5.457	5.314	3.846	3.85	5.231	3.308	2.000
1967	1.059	1.06	1.588	4.676	5.294	1.500	1.54	4.929	2.500	2.357
1968	.571	1.00	.687	3.543	6.343	1.538	1.50	4.538	1.308	2.385
1969	1.000	1.00	1.429	4.036	4.893	1.500	1.50	3.150	2.600	2.450
1970	1.500	1.50	2.417	4.083	5.667	4.208	1.50	5.250	3.958	3.625
1971	2.250	2.11	1.167	3.833	4.875	3.458	3.46	2.958	1.792	3.167
1972	2.107	2.11	1.964	4.286	4.857	5.750	3.46	2.950	3.150	3.300
1973	1.813	1.81	1.938	2.969	5.344	2.875	3.18	3.438	1.938	2.125
1974	1.417	1.42	3.387	2.419	4.484	3.176	3.18	5.294	2.588	2.824
1975	1.357	1.42	3.607	1.893	4.464	6.000	6.00	4.050	3.050	3.300
1976	1.939	1.42	2.909	3.848	5.000	6.333	6.00	5.267	2.000	1.400
1977	1.160	1.69	3.080	2.880	6.080	5.043	5.04	2.957	3.217	3.217
1978	2.286	1.69	1.571	3.371	6.143	4.077	4.08	3.231	3.769	3.077
1979	1.688	1.69	4.969	1.688	4.813	3.875	4.08	3.688	3.875	1.250
1980	3.350	3.35	5.450	2.500	4.500	4.107	3.88	3.679	3.929	2.393
1981	5.542	5.55	4.750	1.917	3.042	3.792	3.79	3.583	2.750	2.417

SOURCE: Calculated as described in this appendix.

Technology and Market Demand

Another possible complication that turned out not to be troublesome was the apparent awkwardness of talking about diesel engines or front-wheel drive as innovations when, in truth, they had already been around for quite some time. How, or so this potential objection ran, could we talk about the market demand for innovation when the things we classified as innovations were not altogether new upon the scene? Our answer was simple: these technologies were new to the engines and drive trains of American-built cars, and they represented design concepts that varied markedly from those that had dominated the U.S. market for decades.

These points aside, our estimates of the market price attached to specific product characteristics are derived from the following equation:

$$P_i = a + \sum_j b_j X_{ij} + u_i$$

where P is the market or transaction price of the i(th) model, a is a constant term, X is the j characteristic of the i model, and u is an error term. The coefficients of the X's (b's) provide an estimate of the market value of the j characteristic.

Because we wanted to get at the value placed by consumers on technology, we had to take into account the effects of production costs, which might bias the coefficients. To do this, we could have built a model of both the demand and supply sides of the market and then used advanced statistical techniques to disentangle the effects of costs and consumer preferences. We chose, however, to follow a simpler course. Since production costs are likely to be more stable than consumer preferences, especially over short periods of time, we decided that differences in the coefficients between the 1977–1978 and 1979–1980 periods were more likely to reflect differences in consumer valuation than in production costs. Further, by including data on list prices in an equation explaining transaction prices, we hoped to gain some additional control for variations in production costs. Our reasoning here was straightforward: list prices are determined by product line policy and by standard costs. They may also reflect a firm's estimate of consumers' valuation, but they will surely include standard costs. We have built equations with and without list prices in order to gauge their effect on our conclusions.

Table C.3 identifies the variables we used in our calculations and provides working definitions for each. Raw data were taken from the appropriate editions of the *Automotive News Digest Data Book,* the *Automotive News Almanac,* the *Red Book,* and *Consumer Reports.* Two of the variables require special comment. In calculating list prices and "year later" prices, we made sure that both applied to vehicles with the same complement of options. For domestic cars, year later prices reflect two different packages of options (package "A":

air conditioning, automatic transmission, radio, and heater; package "B": the "A" list plus power steering). Some cars were available only with the "A" package and some with the "B." For imports, the only option of significance was automatic transmission, and this was relevant only in 1979.

Package efficiency is a measure of internal volume per pound. Figures on vehicle weight are readily available; internal volume was calculated from the data on vehicle dimensions given in *Consumer Reports.* We took the internal volume of both front and rear compartments to be the product of shoulder room and the cross-section area of the compartment.

Table C.4 presents means and standard deviations for all the relevant variables, and table C.5 sets out the estimates generated by the several different versions of our price equation. In the body of the chapter, we make use of the estimates from equation 6, but our general conclusion (that the market valuation of technology changed between 1977–1978 and 1979–1980) is little affected by the choice of equation. Including list prices in the equation does, in fact, alter the magnitude of the coefficients, but it has no effect on the relative change between the two periods. Using F-tests with a 95 percent confidence level, we have rejected the hypothesis that the technology coefficients were identical before and after 1979.

TABLE C.3

Variable Definitions

Variables	Symbols and Definitions
Transaction Price	P_i: one-year-old used-car price of the $i^{(th)}$ model
List Price	P^*: manufacturer's suggested retail price of the $i^{(th)}$ model
Fuel Efficiency	MPG: EPA miles-per-gallon rating for city driving
Driving Range	RNG: MPG $\times$ (reported fuel-tank capacity)
Repair Frequency (two variables entered)	REP1: has value 1 if *Consumer Reports'* survey of repair frequency placed model in "Far Below Average" category; zero otherwise
	REP2: has value 1 if *Consumer Reports'* survey of repair frequency placed model in "Far Above Average" category; zero otherwise
Package Efficiency	VOLWT: internal volume[1] divided by vehicle curb weight
Engine Type	DIESEL: has value 1 if model has diesel engine; zero otherwise
Drive Train	FWD: has value 1 if model has front-wheel drive; zero otherwise
Age of Model	AGE: years since last major model redesign (either in styling or technology)
Size Class	SUBCOMP: has value 1 if model is a subcompact; zero otherwise

NOTE: 1. See the text of this appendix for a definition of internal volume.

146

TABLE C.4

Means and Standard Deviations of Basic Variables (1977 and 1979)

Variable	1977		1979	
	Mean	**Standard Deviation**	**Mean**	**Standard Deviation**
Transaction Price (P$_i$)	$3674	901	$4591	832
List Price (P*)	$4484	1209	$5657	963
Fuel Efficiency (MPG)	21.8	5.3	21.0	4.8
Driving Range (RNG)	318.0	57.7	326.5	70.8
Package Efficiency				
VOLWT (cubic inch per pound)	49.9	7.0	49.3	8.7
Engine Type				
(percent DIESEL)	2.3	14.9	3.5	18.5
Drive Train				
(percent FWD)	25.0	43.3	27.1	44.4
Age of Model (AGE)				
(years)	3.7	3.5	2.5	2.3
Repair Frequency				
(percent)				
REP1	15.9	36.6	3.5	18.5
REP2	22.7	41.9	15.3	36.0
Subcompact				
(percent)	65.9	47.4	50.6	50.0

NOTE: The variables are defined in table C.3.

Technological Diversity

The index of technological diversity is intended to measure variation in market demand for different design concepts, as represented by the market share of production accounted for by each concept. If there are *n* design concepts in the set associated with each design parameter (nature of drive train, for example), and if (*S*1 . . . *Sn*) is the vector of the market share associated with each concept, then the index of diversity *(D)* can be defined as the inverse of the maximum share for a given design parameter.

More formally, we can express the index as:

$$D\max = 1/\max\ (S1\ .\ .\ .\ Sn)$$

In the absence of diversity, production would involve but a single design concept, and *D*max would equal 1. Complete diversity, on the other hand, would be the equal distribution of shares across all concepts for a single parameter, and *D*max would equal *n*.

Data on the share of production accounted for by a given characteristic are presented in table C.6, and these data serve as the basis for the diversity indices

147

TABLE C.5

Estimation-of-Price Equations (1977–1979)

Year/Specification	CONS	SUBCOMP	MPG	RNG	VOLWT	DIESEL	FWD	AGE	P*	REP1	REP2	R²	SEE	d.f.[1]
1977 Results														
1.	4522.0	−1124.0	21.47									.432	730.8	38
	(654.0)	(286.0)	(31.4)											
2.	−132.4	−19.6	20.09						0.74			.873	350.5	37
	(517.0)	(164.3)	(15.06)						(0.07)					
3.	7796.0	−1015.0	69.4		−74.2	−18.3	−204.0	−33.1				.593	653.6	34
	(1527.0)	(274.0)	(38.8)		(34.0)	(874.0)	(421.9)	(30.9)						
4.	165.0	−179.6	37.2		−7.8	−785.7	−148.1	−11.25	0.75			.886	351.3	33
	(1166.0)	(172.9)	(21.1)		(19.6)	(477.1)	(226.8)	(16.8)	(0.08)					
5.	6909.0	−827.1	23.7	3.8	−60.4	−186.0	−251.0	−42.6		−55.0	−106.8	.609	671.3	31
	(1849.0)	(329.0)	(57.6)	(3.4)	(38.5)	(1070.0)	(476.4)	(37.6)		(362.2)	(616.7)			
6.	172.0	−176.7	36.2	0.09	−8.1	−852.6	−315.9	−11.3	0.74	26.0	64.7	.886	367.9	30
	(1283.0)	(195.7)	(31.6)	(1.94)	(22.0)	(1591.5)	(261.5)	(20.9)	(0.09)	(198.8)	(338.6)			
1979 Results														
1.	5814.0	−721.2	10.28									.289	727.5	79
	(592.0)	(195.5)	(21.63)											
2.	−553.1	226.1	31.55						.80			.837	351.1	78
	(486.7)	(111.1)	(10.52)						(0.05)					
3.	7516.0	−460.3	−55.6		28.9	1575.0	1417.0	−70.5				.576	576.7	75
	(685.0)	(186.9)	(25.0)		(12.9)	(426.0)	(231.0)	(30.0)						
4.	483.1	281.3	−0.86		−2.4	308.2	540.6	−35.1	0.71			.878	312.0	74
	(639.4)	(115.1)	(14.1)		(7.2)	(248.9)	(140.9)	(16.4)	(0.05)					
5.	6308.0	−370.7	−88.9	3.9	−9.7	1524.0	998.9	−51.5		−126.6	19.2	.625	553.3	72
	(766.0)	(183.1)	(26.8)	(1.3)	(13.9)	(410.0)	(264.2)	(30.0)		(332.1)	(245.6)			
6.	311.3	312.8	−14.0	1.0	3.4	301.7	416.6	−36.8	0.70	74.4	221.9	.885	309.1	71
	(639.0)	(115.7)	(16.1)	(0.7)	(7.8)	(248.0)	(154.6)	(16.8)	(0.06)	(186.2)	(138.1)			

(Column group heading: **Variables** spans CONS through REP2; **Summary Statistics[1]** spans R², SEE, d.f.)

SOURCE: The dependent variable was the one-year-old price. Each of the equations was estimated using ordinary least squares. In addition to the variables listed here, each equation included variables measuring country of origin—Europe, Japan, and Japan-captive (models produced in Japan, but sold through dealerships of U.S. firms).

NOTES: Standard errors in parentheses. 1. R² = coefficient of determination, SEE = standard error of estimate, d.f. = degrees of freedom.

presented earlier in table 8.2. The sources for table C.6 include *Ward's Auto-motive Yearbook,* 1970–1980, and the April issues (1970–1980) of *Chilton's Automotive Industries, Automotive News Market Data Book,* and *Consumer Reports.*

TABLE C.6

Production Shares of Selected Engine and Drive-Train Characteristics in U.S.-Produced Automobiles (1970–1980)

Characteristic	70	71	72	73	74	Year 75	76	77	78	79	80
I. Engine Parameters											
Cylinder Configuration											
4 Cyl	.02	.08	.06	.07	.12	.09	.07	.06	.13	.22	.29
6 Cyl	.16	.11	.10	.10	.20	.22	.23	.17	.22	.24	.39
8 Cyl	.82	.81	.84	.83	.68	.69	.70	.77	.65	.54	.32
Valve/Camshaft Arrangement											
OHV IL	.18	.19	.16	.17	.31	.30	.27	.18	.25	.16	.23
OHC IL	.00	.00	.00	.00	.00	.00	.00	.00	.00	.17	.18
OHV V	.82	.81	.84	.83	.69	.70	.73	.82	.75	.67	.59
Fuel											
Diesel	.00	.00	.00	.00	.00	.00	.00	.00	.00	.00	.03
Gasoline	1.00	1.00	1.00	1.00	1.00	1.00	1.00	1.00	1.00	1.00	.97
Fuel Delivery											
1 Bbl	.17	.19	.16	.15	.27	.28	.22	.14	.15	.12	.10
2 Bbl	.61	.59	.60	.65	.53	.52	.62	.65	.72	.59	.77
EFI	.00	.00	.00	.00	.00	.01	.00	.01	.01	.09	.05
4 Bbl	.22	.22	.18	.20	.20	.19	.16	.20	.12	.18	.07
Turbo 2	.00	.00	.00	.00	.00	.00	.00	.00	.00	.00	.00
Turbo 4	.00	.00	.00	.00	.00	.00	.00	.00	.00	.00	.01
II. Drive-Train Parameters											
Wheels-Driven											
FWD	.00	.01	.01	.01	.01	.01	.01	.01	.07	.10	.23
RWD	1.00	.99	.99	.99	.99	.99	.99	.99	.93	.89	.76
4WD	.00	.00	.00	.00	.00	.00	.00	.00	.00	.01	.01
Engine Orientation											
Transverse	.00	.00	.00	.00	.00	.00	.00	.00	.04	.09	.21
Longitudinal	1.00	1.00	1.00	1.00	1.00	1.00	1.00	1.00	.96	.91	.79

SOURCE: See the text of this appendix.
NOTE: The following definitions are used in the table.
OHV IL: overhead valve—in line; OHC IL: overhead cam—in line; OHV V: overhead valve—V-configuration; Bbl: barrel; EFI: electronic fuel injection; Turbo: turbocharger; FWD: front-wheel drive; RWD: rear-wheel drive; 4WD: four-wheel drive.

Appendix D

Innovation in the

U.S. Automobile Industry

from 1893 to 1981

Sources

Our objective was to generate a chronological listing of product and process innovations that could be used to gain a better sense of the impact of new technology on competition. We sought, therefore, the earliest significant commercial introduction of each innovation. As a starting point, we examined the information contained in various popular accounts of the auto industry. For the early years we also consulted Abernathy's *The Productivity Dilemma;* the Federal Trade Commission's 1939 *Report On The Motor Vehicle Industry* (particularly pp. 907–919); Arthur Pound's history of the first thirty years of General Motors, *The Turning Wheel* (Garden City, NY: Doubleday, Doran & Co., 1934); Allan Nevins's three-part series on the Ford Motor Company; and specific company histories of Buick, Cadillac, Hudson, Oldsmobile, Packard, and Studebaker.

Richard Fabris's *A Study of Product Innovation in the Automobile Industry During the Period 1919–1962* (Ph. D. diss., University of Illinois, 1966) also provided information on new technology, as did the following articles: "A Decade of Automotive Development," *Automotive Industries* (January 15, 1940); the Silver Anniversary Issue of the *Automobile Trade Journal* (December

1924); a twelve-part series on the engineering evolution of the automobile industry that appeared monthly in *Car Life* from July, 1964, to June, 1965; and "An Encyclopedia of Automotive Facts" that appeared in *Motor Trend* in March, 1964. Lawrence J. White's *The Automobile Industry Since 1945* contains information on the present period, as does the fourth edition of *Automobiles of America,* a publication of the Motor Vehicle Manufacturers Association of America.

Organization of the Data Base

To facilitate handling of the data, we transferred all information collected to note cards according to the following format:

A. Year

Product innovations were entered according to their model year introduction date. Since it became clear that the distinction between model year and calendar year was not strictly observed by motor vehicle producers prior to 1925, we treated both as equivalent. All innovations relating to process and assembly were entered according to their calendar year date of introduction.

B. Manufacturer

Whenever possible we listed the divisional name and/or the corporate name of the original equipment manufacturer—with certain exceptions:

1. In a few areas, notably the production of tires and some all-steel bodies, the auto companies have historically relied on external suppliers for their component requirements. Accordingly, some of the product innovations in these areas have the supplier's name entered as the manufacturer. Whenever possible, however, we listed both the name of the supplier and the name of the original equipment manufacturer who pioneered the first significant commercial introduction of the product or process. An example of this would be the introduction of Budd's all-steel body on the Hupmobile and Oakland in 1912. Use of a combined supplier's and originating car producer's name often conceals a time lag between the supplier's market introduction and the first automotive application. The use of tubeless tires on the 1955 Packard, for example, denotes their initial appearance as original equipment but does not account for the fact

that the tires were available from the firm that invented them—B.F. Goodrich—as an after-market item as early as 1948. To account for this factor, we give the data on the first supplier introduction in parentheses.

2. We consider only U.S. manufacturers. Although we explored the European antecedents of various products and processes, the data base excludes foreign makes and overseas production by American firms.

3. In general, we also excluded product and process innovations that appeared on specialty cars, racing vehicles, or prototypes and experimental automobiles.

C. Innovation

This listing contains the first significant commercial introduction or application of an innovation. We provide additional explanatory or peripheral information relating to function or use in parentheses.

Ranking System

After compiling a chronological listing of automobile innovations by firm from 1893 to the present, we then grouped the entries into one of four categories as follows:

A. Drive Train

Includes engine, transmission, clutch, drive shaft, rear axle, and related components. Some examples of innovations in this category would be the first large scale production of the high-speed V-8 engine by Cadillac in 1915; the introduction of the Synchromesh transmission by General Motors in 1928; and the development of the alternator in 1958 by Chrysler and Ford.

B. Process and Assembly

Contains all innovations directly related to the manufacturing process, including new machinery and equipment, new production techniques such as casting and other foundry methods, and new materials uses. Some examples of innovations in this category would be the introduction of electric spot welding by

Budd in 1912 and of the thin-wall, gray cast-iron cylinder block engine by Ford in 1959.

C. Body and Chassis

Includes frame, suspension, brakes, springs, steering, front end parts, chassis lubrication, wheels and tires, and body panels. Some examples of innovations in this group would be Chrysler's introduction of power steering in 1951, and the appearance of ball-joint, front-wheel suspension by the Lincoln Division of Ford in 1953.

D. Other

All miscellaneous items such as exterior trim parts, instrumentation, seats, and many safety-related items like sidedoor impact protection and shoulder harnesses.

Weighting

Our next step in the development of the data base was to weight each item using as a unit of analysis the overall impact of the innovation on the production process. We chose a seven-point transilience scale because it gave us enough latitude to judge between innovations with little or no impact on the production process, which we coded as 1's, and those very disruptive for products or processes, which we coded as 7's.

Methodology

Table D.1 presents a chronological listing of the assembled innovations from 1893 through 1981. Table D.2 displays data on the transilience of these innovations over time. Since the number of years covered by the data is very large and the number of innovations in each year small, we have defined groups of three-year periods signified by the center year (some of the groups contain more than three years, notably during the early years of the industry). These groups are designated epochs. For each observation in an epoch, the 1–7 weight has been squared to enhance the range between incremental and epochal innovations. Finally, we summed the squared weights across the epoch in each category to arrive at a final score. To highlight trends in the data, the twenty-nine scores in each category, representing the (roughly) twenty-nine three-year epochs since 1893, were smoothed using a simple median-removal technique. (For a description of the technique, see John W. Tukey, *Exploratory Data Analysis* [Reading, Mass.: Addison-Wesley, 1977] pp. 205–230.) Alternative weighting schemes lead to similiar results.

TABLE D.1

Automotive Innovations 1893–1981

#	Year	Producer(s)	Innovation	Rank	Category
1	1893	Duryea	Differential Rear Axle	4	1
2	1893	Duryea	Electric Spark Ignition Battery	3	1
3	1893	Duryea	Muffler	1	1
4	1893	Duryea	Single Plate Clutch	4	1
5	1893	Duryea	Spray Type Carburetor (replaced mixing valve)	3	1
6	1895	Duryea (Hartford Rubber Works [supplier])	Pneumatic Tires	2	3
7	1895	Haynes-Apperson	Aluminum Engine	5	1
8	1896	Duryea	First Multiple Production of One Car Design (13 vehicles)	6	2
9	1896	King	En-Bloc Engine	5	1
10	1896	King	Four-Cylinder Engine on a Production Car	3	1
11	1896	Munson	Automatic Starter Using Electricity	1	1
12	1896	Winton	Compressed Air Self-Starter	1	1
13	1896	Winton	Two Seat Car	1	3
14	1898	Columbia Electric	Electric Lights (parabolic reflector headlamps)	2	4
15	1898	Columbia Electric	Enclosed Car Body (wood and steel)	4	3
16	1898	Duryea	Internal-Expanding Brakes	4	3
17	1898	Franklin	Air-Cooled, 4-Cylinder Valve-in-Head Engine	2	1
18	1898	Haynes	Nickel-Steel Components	2	2
19	1899	B.F. Goodrich (supplier)	Clincher Tire	1	3
20	1899	Mobile Steamer	Center Steering	4	3
21	1899	Packard	Automatic Spark Advance	4	1
22	1900	Most Producers	Gasoline Engine Mounted in Front of Car	4	2
23	1900	Duryea	Remy-Built Ignition Dynamo	3	1
24	1900	G and J Jeffrey	Left-Hand Control	3	3
25	1900	Knox	Single-Cylinder, Air-Cooled Engine	3	1

NOTE: The numbers under Rank are the transilience scores assigned to each innovation as described in the text. The numbers under Category indicate the technical system affected by the innovation; four categories are used: drive train (1), process (2), body and chassis (3), and other (4).

Automotive Innovations 1893–1981

#	Year	Producer(s)	Innovation	Rank	Category
26	1900	Orient Auto; Packard	Steering Wheel (replaced tiller)	4	3
27	1900	R.E. Dietz (supplier)	Kerosene Lamp	1	4
28	1901	Autocar	First Shaft-Driven American Car	5	1
29	1901	Autocar	Spark Coil for Ignition	2	1
30	1901	Automobile Co. of America	Six-Cylinder Engine	3	1
31	1901	Elmore	Electric Side and Tail-lights	1	4
32	1901	Oldsmobile	Jones-Built Speedometer	1	4
33	1901	Oldsmobile	Nickel Plating of Trim Parts (replaced brass)	1	2
34	1901	Oldsmobile	World's First Mass-Produced Automobile (Curved-Dash Runabout)	7	2
35	1901	Peerless; Ward-Leonard	Gearshift Lever Mounted on the Steering Column	2	3
36	1901	Winton	Apple-Built Stabilized Battery (replaced dry cells)	2	1
37	1902	Autocar	Spark Plug with Porcelain Insulation	2	1
38	1902	Electric Vehicle Co.	Elliott's Steering Knuckle	4	3
39	1902	Haynes-Apperson	Holtzer-Cabot Magneto Generator	3	1
40	1902	Locomobile	Cellular Radiator	2	1
41	1902	Locomobile	4-Cylinder, Front-Mounted Engine (water-cooled)	4	1
42	1902	Marmon	Air-Cooled, V-4 Engine	2	1
43	1902	Marmon	First All-Metal Body (aluminum casting)	5	2
44	1902	Briscoe (supplier)	Siphon Cooling	2	1
45	1902	Northern	Planetary Gearset Transmission	5	1
46	1902	Northern	Running Boards	2	3
47	1902	Northern	Three-Point Suspension of Power Unit	5	1
48	1902	Northern	Unit Powerplant (integral engine and transmission unit)	5	1
49	1902	Northern; Peerless	Universal Joint	3	1
50	1902	Packard	Four-Position "H" Slot Transmission	3	1
51	1902	Peerless	Mercedes-Type Hood (coil radiator vertically mounted in front of car)	2	3

Automotive Innovations 1893–1981

#	Year	Producer(s)	Innovation	Rank	Category
52	1903	A.O. Smith (supplier) for Peerless	Pressed Steel Frames	5	3
53	1903	Goodyear (supplier)	First Straight-Side Tire	3	3
54	1903	Marmon	Forced Feed Engine Lubrication	3	1
55	1903	Marmon	Side Entrance Tonneau Body	1	3
56	1903	Northern	Windshield	2	4
57	1903	Oldsmobile; Peerless; Rambler	Mechanically Operated Intake Valves	2	1
58	1903	Peerless	Steel Cylinder Liners	2	1
59	1903	Postal	Car Heater	1	4
60	1903	Union	Earliest Friction Transmission (eliminated the use of gears; utilized a friction wheel)	3	1
61	1903	Winton	First Straight Eight-Cylinder Engine	3	1
62	1904	Apperson; Packard	First Expanding-Band Clutch	2	1
63	1904	Autocar	Circulating Motor Lubrication System	2	1
64	1904	Ford	Torque Tube Drive	4	1
65	1904	Franklin	Die-Casting First Used in Car Production	2	2
66	1904	Peerless	Cone Clutch	3	1
67	1904	Pierce-Arrow	First Pressure Lubrication System (with an oil pump)	2	1
68	1904	Sturtevant Brothers	Early Automatic Transmission	3	1
69	1904	Sturtevant Brothers	"Power" Air Brakes	2	3
70	1904	Trufault-Hartford (supplier)	Shock Absorbers	2	3
71	1904	Welch	Hemispherical Combustion Cylinder Head	3	1
72	1905	Apple (supplier) on Stoddard-Dayton	Battery Timer and Distributor	2	1
73	1905	Goodyear (supplier)	Universal Rim	1	3
74	1905	Northern	Dual Muffler System	1	1
75	1905	Peerless	Cape or Folding Top (displaced canopy top)	1	3
76	1905	Weed (supplier)	Tire Chains	1	3
77	1906	Buick	Storage Battery	1	1
78	1906	Ford	Wiring Harness for Electrical System	4	1
79	1906	Franklin	Fender with Inside Mud Guard	1	3

Automotive Innovations 1893–1981

#	Year	Producer(s)	Innovation	Rank	Category
80	1906	Knight and Kilbourne	Sleeve Valves	2	1
81	1907	Columbia; Matheson; Stearns	Twin Carburetors	1	1
82	1907	Firestone (supplier)	Non-Skid Tire Tread Design	1	3
83	1907	Ford	Electrical Resistance Welding	3	2
84	1907	Ford	Multiple Simultaneous Machining Operations on Cast Parts	5	2
85	1907	Ford	Stamped Crankcase Pans	2	2
86	1907	Ford	Integrally Cast Cylinder Block and Crankcase	5	2
87	1907	Northern	Pneumatic Clutch	2	1
88	1907	Reo	Rumble Seat	1	3
89	1908	Columbia	Magnetic Clutch	1	1
90	1908	Ford	Gear-Driven Fan	2	1
91	1908	Ford	Magneto Integrated into Flywheel	6	1
92	1908	Ford	Detachable Cylinder Heads	6	1
93	1908	Ford	Spark and Throttle Control	2	1
94	1908	Ford	Vanadium Steel Components	4	2
95	1909	Ford	Steel Running Boards (replaced wood)	2	2
96	1909	Howard Co. (supplier) on Winton	Demountable Rims	1	3
97	1909	Hupmobile	Controlled Gravity Engine Lubrication	2	1
98	1909	Jones (supplier)	First Practical Battery Hydrometer	1	4
99	1909	Klaxon (supplier)	Motor-Driven Electric Horn	1	4
100	1909	Knight	Silent (toothed) Timing Chains	1	1
101	1910	Adams-Farwell	Early Fuel Injection System	4	1
102	1910	B.F. Goodrich (supplier)	Cord Tire	2	3
103	1910	Fisher Body Co. on Cadillac (GM)	Closed Body (150 units ordered)	2	3
104	1910	Ford	Industry's First Branch Assembly Plant (Kansas City, Missouri)	7	2
105	1910	King; Owen	Gearshift Mounted on Center of Gearbox	1	3
106	1911	Columbia; Stearns; Stoddard-Dayton	Knight Sleeve-Valve Engine	2	1

Automotive Innovations 1893–1981

#	Year	Producer(s)	Innovation	Rank	Category
107	1911	Hudson	Simplified Chassis	2	3
108	1911	Levett Co. (supplier)	Aluminum Alloy Pistons for Automotive Use	3	1
109	1911	Locomobile	Spare Tire in Rear of Car	1	4
110	1911	Marmon (racing version)	Oil Pressure Dash Gauge	1	4
111	1911	Marmon (racing version)	Rear-View Mirror	1	4
112	1911	Metz	Early Disc Brake System	3	3
113	1912	Boyce (supplier)	Engine Temperature Indicator ("Moto-Meter")	1	4
114	1912	Budd (supplier)	Electric Spot Welding (on all-steel car)	4	2
115	1912	Budd Design on Hupmobile; Oakland (GM)	All-Steel Open Car Body	6	3
116	1912	Cadillac (GM)	Electric Starter	4	1
117	1912	Cadillac (GM)	Generator-Battery (for lighting and ignition)	3	1
118	1913	Ford	Moving Flywheel Magneto Assembly Line (at Highland Park)	5	2
119	1913	Ford	Planetary Transmission Mounted Directly on Crankshaft	2	2
120	1913	Goodyear (supplier)	Tire Casing of Overlapping Cord Material (tripled useful tire life)	1	3
121	1913	Hudson	Cabriolet-Type Body (coupe with a folding top)	2	3
122	1913	Hudson	Sedan-Type Body	4	3
123	1913	Kelsey (supplier)	Steel Felloe for Wood-Spoked Wheel	2	2
124	1913	Kissel	Wrap-Around Windshield	1	4
125	1913	Monarch	Radiator under Hood	2	3
126	1913	Packard	Spiral Bevel Gear (noiseless rear axle)	4	1
127	1913	Spaulding	Seats Whose Backs Fold Down to Form a Bed	1	4
128	1913	Studebaker	First Production Six-Cylinder Engine Cast in a Single Block of Gray Cast Iron (model E-6)	4	1
129	1914	Cadillac (GM)	First Large-Scale Production V-8 Engine (water-cooled; high speed; type 51)	7	1

Automotive Innovations 1893–1981

#	Year	Producer(s)	Innovation	Rank	Category
130	1914	Dodge	Mass Production of All-Steel Open Car Body	4	2
131	1914	Ford	Elevated, Moving Chassis Assembly Line (at Highland Park)	7	2
132	1914	Packard	Hand Brake at Driver's Left	1	4
133	1914	Packard	Helicon or Curved-Tooth Bevel Gears	3	1
134	1914	Pierce-Arrow	Front and Rear Collision Bumpers	3	3
135	1914	Stewart-Warner (supplier)	Vacuum-Operated Fuel System	2	1
136	1914	Studebaker	Dash-Mounted Gasoline Engine Gauge	1	4
137	1915	Briscoe	"Cyclops-Eye" Headlight	1	4
138	1915	Cadillac (GM)	Adjustable Steering Wheel	1	3
139	1915	Cadillac (GM)	Tilt-Beam Headlights	2	4
140	1915	Cadillac (GM)	Thermostatic Water Circulation Control	2	1
141	1915	Entz on Owen	Electric Differential Transmission	3	1
142	1915	Ford	Continuous Process Flat Glass Plant	3	2
143	1915	Franklin	Spare Tire in Trunk	1	4
144	1915	Maxwell	Adjustable Driver's Seat	1	4
145	1916	Briscoe; Owen	Convertible Roadster (rear top storage)	2	3
146	1916	Haynes and Norwalk (supplier) on Premier	Solenoid Magnets for Gear Shifting in Sliding Gear Transmission	2	1
147	1916	Hudson	Counter-Balancing of Crankshaft in Multi-Cylinder (6) Engine	4	1
148	1916	Kissel; Kline; Packard; Winton	"Sociable Body" (aisle between two front seats)	1	3
149	1916	Locomobile	Locking Control of Lighting and Ignition	1	4
150	1916	Packard	Aluminum Alloy Pistons	3	1
151	1916	Packard	First Production Model V-12 Engine	2	1
152	1917	Ford	Baked Enamel Finishes	6	2
153	1917	Motor Wheel Corp. (supplier)	Stamped Steel Disc Wheel	3	2
154	1917	Paige	V-Type Windshield	1	4
155	1917	Studebaker	Internal Manifold "Hot Spot" on the Intake Manifold	4	1

160

Automotive Innovations 1893–1981

#	Year	Producer(s)	Innovation	Rank	Category
156	1918	Mercer	Double-Acting Hydraulic Shock Absorber	1	3
157	1919	Franklin	Electric Vaporizer in the Carburetor	2	1
158	1920	Daniels	Golf Bag Attachment (over the running board)	1	4
159	1920	Ford	Continuous Pouring of Molten Iron	4	2
160	1920	Ford	Integral Brake Drum and Wheel Hub	3	2
161	1920	Ford	Molds Moved by Conveyor to Molten Metal Pouring Station	3	2
162	1920	Kissel	Bullet-Shaped Headlamps	1	4
163	1920	Packard	Alemite Chassis Lubrication	2	4
164	1920	Packard	Lanchester Vibration Dampener (first American use)	4	1
165	1921	Buick (GM); McFarlan	Solid Metal Wheels	2	3
166	1921	Duesenberg	Four-Wheel Mechanical Brakes	3	3
167	1921	Duesenberg; Kenworthy	Straight-Eight (or in-line) Engine (first major American use)	4	1
168	1921	Ford	Continuous Strip Plate Glass Casting	1	2
169	1921	Wills-Sainte Claire	Back-Up Lights	1	4
170	1921	Wills-Sainte Claire	Nickel-Molybdenum Steel	2	2
171	1922	A.O. Smith for GM	Mechanical Transfer in Building Automobile Frames	5	2
172	1922	Duesenberg	Four-Wheel Hydraulic Brakes	4	3
173	1922	Duesenberg	Overhead Camshaft Engine	4	1
174	1922	Ford	Plastic Steering Wheel	1	2
175	1922	Hudson	Inexpensive Closed Car Built of Wood and Steel	7	3
176	1922	Hudson	Sliding Bench Seat	1	4
177	1922	Nash	Rubber Engine Mounts	5	1
178	1922	Rickenbacker	Air Cleaner	1	1
179	1923	Cadillac (GM)	Thermostatic Carburetion Control	4	1
180	1923	Chandler	Traffic Transmission	2	1
181	1923	Dodge	All-Steel, Closed Sedan Car Body	5	3

Automotive Innovations 1893–1981

#	Year	Producer(s)	Innovation	Rank	Category
182	1923	Firestone on Ford	First Low-Pressure Balloon Tires	2	3
183	1923	GM	(Tetra) Ethyl Anti-Knock Gasoline	4	4
184	1923	Oldsmobile (GM)	Sectionalized Body Production	5	2
185	1923	Packard	Cigar Lighter	1	4
186	1923	Star	First Production Station Wagon	2	3
187	1924	Cadillac (GM)	Balanced V-Type 8-Cylinder Engine (counterweighted crankshaft)	5	1
188	1924	Cadillac (GM)	Crankcase Ventilation	5	1
189	1924	Ford	Automatic Spring Forming Machine	2	2
190	1924	Ford	Constant Temperature Inspection Rooms	2	2
191	1924	GM	Harmonic Crankshaft Balancer	4	2
192	1924	Oakland (GM)	Lacquer Paint Finish (DUCO-Pyroxolin)	6	2
193	1924	Packard	Mass-Produced Straight-8 L-Head Engine	2	1
194	1924	Springfield Body Corp.	Factory-Installed Radio	1	4
195	1925	Budd (supplier)	Automatic Welding Equipment	5	2
196	1925	Buick (GM)	Power Windshield Wipers	1	4
197	1925	Chrysler	High Compression L-Head Engine	4	1
198	1925	Chrysler	Replaceable, Cartridge Oil Filter outside the Engine	2	1
199	1925	Delco (GM)	Piston-Type Hydraulic Shock Absorber	1	3
200	1925	Ford	Pyroxolin Paints in Multicolors	4	2
201	1925	Oldsmobile (GM)	Chrome Plating (replaced nickel)	2	2
202	1925	Studebaker	Duplex Body Type (steel accessory top)	2	3
203	1926	A.C. (GM)	Cam-Operated Mechanical Fuel Pump	2	1
204	1926	Saginaw for Cadillac (GM)	Worm-and-Roller Steering Gear	3	3
205	1926	Chrysler	Engine Isolated from Frame	4	3

Innovation in the U.S. Automobile Industry from 1893 to 1981

Automotive Innovations 1893–1981

#	Year	Producer(s)	Innovation	Rank	Category
206	1926	Ford	Drop Center Wheel Rims (replaced demountable rims on tire)	2	3
207	1926	Oakland (GM)	L-6 Engine (begins low stroke-to-bore ratio trend)	5	1
208	1926	Rickenbacker; Stutz	Safety Glass	1	4
209	1927	Chrysler	Flexible Rubber Engine Mounts	2	1
210	1927	Chrysler	Rubber Spring Shackles	1	3
211	1927	Ford	Mercury Vapor Plant Lighting	1	2
212	1927	GM	Foot-Controlled Dimmer Switch	1	4
213	1927	Hudson	Starter Button on Dash	1	4
214	1927	Packard	Hypoid Gears in Rear Axle	5	1
215	1928	Ford	Seam Welding Method	4	2
216	1928	GM	Tungsten Carbide Cutting Tools (first American automotive use)	4	2
217	1928	Hudson	Natural Grip Steering Wheel	1	3
218	1928	Studebaker	Single Stud-Type Frame Mounting for Radiator and Fender	2	3
219	1928	Warner (supplier) on Paige	4-Speed Internal Gear Transmission	3	1
220	1929	Auburn; Cord	X-Shaped Crossmember Frame	4	3
221	1929	Cadillac (GM)	"Synchromesh" Transmission	3	1
222	1929	Chandler	Westinghouse Vacuum Brakes	1	3
223	1929	Ford	Car Disassembly and Scrapping Plant	1	2
224	1929	GM	Tungsten Carbide "Tipped" Cutting Tools	3	2
225	1930	Cadillac (GM)	Automatic Hydraulic Tappet Clearance Adjusters/Silencers	2	1
226	1930	Chrysler	Stromberg-Supplied Downdraft Carburetor	4	1
227	1930	Cord	Front-Wheel Drive	3	1
228	1930	Firestone (supplier)	High Speed, Highway Travel Tire	1	3
229	1931	Buick (GM); Hupmobile	Oil Cooler	2	1
230	1931	Cadillac (GM)	Automatic Control for 2-Speed Transmission	2	1

163

Automotive Innovations 1893–1981

#	Year	Producer(s)	Innovation	Rank	Category
231	1931	Cadillac (GM)	V-16 Engine	2	1
232	1931	Chrysler	"Floating Power"	2	1
233	1931	Ford	Dual Downdraft Carburetor (2-barrel)	2	1
234	1931	Graham-Paige	Rubber-Cushioned Chassis Spring	2	3
235	1931	Oldsmobile (GM)	Automatic Manifold Heat Control	3	1
236	1931	Pontiac (GM)	Pressed Steel Axle Housing	1	2
237	1931	Pontiac (GM)	Tin-Plating of Cast Iron Pistons	2	2
238	1931	Studebaker	Carburetor Intake Silencer	1	1
239	1931	Studebaker	"Free-Wheeling" Transmission	3	1
240	1931	Studebaker	Vacuum Spark Advance	3	1
241	1932	Chrysler	Cast Iron Brake Drums for Passenger Cars	2	3
242	1932	Chrysler	Vacuum and Centrifugal Spark Advance (first use of this combination)	2	1
243	1932	Chrysler	Valve-Seat Inserts in Cast Iron Cylinder Blocks	4	1
244	1932	Ford	Hydraulic Transfer Machine (to connect two boring operations on a V-8 engine)	5	2
245	1932	Ford	Mass-Produced, Low-Cost V-8 Engine Cast En-Bloc	5	2
246	1932	Graham	Aluminum Cylinder Heads	3	1
247	1932	Hudson	Proferall Camshaft	3	1
248	1932	Oldsmobile (GM)	Stromberg-Suppled Automatic Choke	3	1
249	1932	Pontiac (GM)	Pressed Steel Radiator Grille	1	2
250	1932	Reo	Windshield Pillars Rounded into Car Roof	2	4
251	1933	Buick (GM); Hudson	Vacuum-Operated Clutch	2	1
252	1933	Chrysler	Roller Bearing Universal Joint	2	1
253	1933	Ford	Portable Assembly Line Power Tools	3	2
254	1933	Ford	Synthetic Resin Baked Enamel Finish	2	2
255	1933	Graham	Full Skirted Front Fenders	1	3
256	1933	Nash	Directional Turn Signals	1	4
257	1934	Buick (GM)	Accelerator Pedal	1	4
258	1934	Chrysler	One-Piece, Curved Glass Windshield	2	4

Automotive Innovations 1893–1981

#	Year	Producer(s)	Innovation	Rank	Category
259	1934	Chrysler	Forward Engine Mounting nearly over Front Wheel Centers	3	3
260	1934	DeSoto; Chrysler	Airflow Streamlining	4	3
261	1934	Ford	Automatic Inspection Machines	3	2
262	1934	Ford	Cast Alloy Steel Crankshaft	4	2
263	1934	Ford	Cast Camshaft (using a controlled chill method of hardening cam tips)	3	2
264	1934	Ford	Continuous V-8 Engine Casting Line (using a monoblock casting process)	7	2
265	1934	GM	Knee-Action Independent Front Wheel Suspension (two design types used)	6	3
266	1934	Fisher (GM)	"No-Draft Ventilation"	2	3
267	1934	Graham	Centrifugal Supercharger	2	1
268	1934	Reo	"Self Shifter"	3	1
269	1935	Borg-Warner (supplier) on Chrysler	Automatic Overdrive Transmission	4	1
270	1935	Cadillac (GM)	High Output Generator and Regulator	2	1
271	1935	Chevrolet (GM)	Double-Articulated Brake Shoes	1	3
272	1935	Chrysler	Synchronized Front and Rear Springs (for anti-pitch ride)	2	3
273	1935	Chrysler	Tubular Frame Seats	1	4
274	1935	Ford	Heat Drying Lamps for Painting (reduced drying time to five minutes)	3	2
275	1935	Ford	Faster Rolling Speeds in Strip Steelmaking	2	2
276	1935	GM	Turret Top (first all-steel, outer shell top supported by wooden rails)	4	3
277	1935	Goodyear (supplier)	"Life Guard" Blowout Proof Inner Tube	1	3
278	1935	Hudson	Rear Trunk Made Integral Part of Body	1	3
279	1935	Reo	Gear Shift on Dash	1	4
280	1935	Studebaker	"Planar" Front Wheel Suspension	4	3
281	1936	Chevrolet (GM)	First All-Steel Station Wagon Body	2	3

Automotive Innovations 1893–1981

#	Year	Producer(s)	Innovation	Rank	Category
282	1936	Ford	Transfer Machines for Drive Train Parts (Baird Machine Company supplier)	4	2
283	1936	Hudson; Terraplane	"Electric Hand" Preselect Transmission	2	1
284	1936	Lincoln (Ford)	Alligator Hood (rear-hinged, front opening)	1	3
285	1936	Lincoln (Ford)	Semi-Unit Construction Body	5	2
286	1936	Studebaker	Budd-Built Monopiece All-Steel Roof with no Wooden Inner Supports	2	3
287	1937	Chrysler	Built-In Defroster Vents	1	4
288	1937	Hudson	Double Automatic Emergency Brake System (separate reserve unit)	1	3
289	1937	Hudson	Steel Torque Steering Arm	2	3
290	1937	Studebaker	"Hill-Holder" Brake	1	3
291	1938	Buick (GM)	Horn Ring	1	4
292	1938	Buick (GM); Oldsmobile (GM)	Safety Transmission	3	1
293	1938	Chevrolet (GM)	Automated Forge Shop	3	2
294	1938	Chrysler	Front Seat that Moves Up and Down as Well as Back and Forth	1	4
295	1938	Chrysler	Fully Rubber Insulated Body Mounts	2	3
296	1938	Chrysler	Safety Padding on Back of Front Seat	1	4
297	1938	Chrysler	"Superfinish"	2	2
298	1938	GM	Automatic Dome Light Switch	1	4
299	1938	Goodyear (supplier)	Rayon Cord Tire	1	3
300	1938	Packard	Air Conditioning Optional	2	4
301	1938	Perfect Circle (supplier)	Piston Rings with Chemical Treatment on Surface	1	1
302	1939	Buick (GM)	Rear Coil Spring Suspension	3	3
303	1939	Buick (GM)	Vacuum-Operated Convertible Top	1	4
304	1939	Chevrolet (GM)	Vacuum-Operated Gearshift	1	1
305	1939	Chrysler	Fluid or Hydraulic Coupling (replaced mechanical flywheel)	5	1
306	1939	Chrysler	Rubber Insulated Steering Gear	2	3

166

Automotive Innovations 1893–1981

#	Year	Producer(s)	Innovation	Rank	Category
307	1939	Hudson	Safety Hood Latch (hinged in front)	1	3
308	1939	Nash	"Conditioned Air" Heating and Ventilation System	2	4
309	1939	Pontiac (GM)	Duflex Rear Springs	2	3
310	1939	Pontiac (GM)	Manual Gear Shifting Device	2	1
311	1940	Cadillac (GM) (Saginaw [supplier])	Recirculating-Ball Steering Gear	3	3
312	1940	Hudson	"Airfoam" Seat Cushions	1	4
313	1940	Lincoln (Ford)	Omitted Running Boards	1	3
314	1940	Most Producers	Sealed Beam Headlamps	1	4
315	1940	Oldsmobile (GM)	"Hydra-Matic" Automatic Transmission	7	1
316	1940	Pontiac (GM)	Torpedo Coupe Body	2	3
317	1941	Budd Design on Nash	All-Steel, Single Unit Body (integral body and frame)	7	3
318	1941	Most Producers	Hydraulic Window Lifts	1	4
319	1941	Chrysler	Safety Rim Wheel	1	3
320	1941	Chrysler	Two Cylinders in Front Brakes	1	3
321	1941	Chrysler	Two-Speed Electric Windshield Wipers	1	4
322	1941	Lincoln (Ford)	Power Seats	1	4
323	1941	Oldsmobile; Pontiac (GM)	6- or 8-Cylinder Engine Commonality	5	2
324	1942	Buick (GM)	Compound Carburetion	2	1
325	1942	DeSoto (Chrysler)	Concealed Headlamps	1	4
326	1942	Packard	Electrically Controlled Clutch	1	1
327	1945	GM	Teletype within Assembly	2	2
328	1946	Chrysler	Hardtop Convertible	2	3
329	1947	Chevrolet (GM)	Overhead Assembly Line (Flint, Michigan and Van Nuys, California plants)	3	2
330	1947	Chrysler	First Full Flow Oil Filter	1	1
331	1947	Ford (Excello [supplier])	8 Stations in Engine Machining Line	3	2
332	1947	Goodyear (supplier)	Nylon Cord Tires	1	3
333	1947	Kaiser-Fraser	Gas Tank Located beneath License Plate	1	4
334	1947	Studebaker	Self-Adjusting Brakes	2	3
335	1948	Buick (GM)	19 Station Cylinder-Block Machining Line	3	2
336	1948	Hudson	"Monobilt" Step Down Body and Frame	5	3
337	1948	Packard	Power-Operated Windows	1	4

Automotive Innovations 1893–1981

#	Year	Producer(s)	Innovation	Rank	Category
338	1948	Studebaker	Candalon Nylon Cord Upholstery	1	4
339	1949	Buick (GM)	"Dynaflow" Improved Automatic Transmission	5	1
340	1949	Buick; Cadillac; Oldsmobile (GM)	Double-Curved Windshield	1	4
341	1949	Buick; Cadillac Oldsmobile (GM)	Pillarless Hardtop Convertible	1	3
342	1949	Cadillac (GM)	Rear-End Tail Fins	1	3
343	1949	Cadillac; Oldsmobile (GM)	Short-Stroke, High Compression V-8 Engine with Overhead Valves and Hydraulic Lifters	4	1
344	1949	Crosley	Exhaust Valve Rotator	2	1
345	1950	Buick (GM)	Computer Applied to Assembly Plant Scheduling	3	2
346	1950	Chevrolet (GM); Chrysler; Crosley	Bonded Brakes	2	3
347	1950	Chrysler	Combination Ignition and Starter Actuated by a Key	1	1
348	1950	Chrysler	Safety Cushion Dash Panel	2	4
349	1950	Chrysler; Crosley	Disc Brakes	4	3
350	1950	Ford	Automated Stamping Press and Welding Machine Lines (for body parts)	5	2
351	1950	Ford	Cathodic Etching for Microscopic Inspection	2	2
352	1950	Ford	Overhead Engine Conveyor	2	2
353	1950	Kaiser	Fold-Away Rear Seat Cargo Area	1	4
354	1951	Buick (GM)	Tinted Non-Glare Glass	1	4
355	1951	Chrysler	All-Electric Window Controls	1	4
356	1951	Chrysler	Hemihead V-8 Engine	5	1
357	1951	Ford	Cleveland Engine Plant	7	2
358	1951	Kaiser	Narrow Windshield Corner Posts and Safety Pop-Out Windshield	1	4
359	1951	Kaiser	Padded Dash (with recessed instruments)	1	4
360	1951	Lincoln (Ford); Nash-Kelvinator	One-Piece Curved Windshield	1	4
361	1951	Nash-Kelvinator	Plastic-Insulated Ignition System	1	1
362	1951	Nash-Kelvinator	Seat Belts	1	4
363	1952	Chrysler	"Hydraguide" Power Steering	3	3

Automotive Innovations 1893–1981

#	Year	Producer(s)	Innovation	Rank	Category
364	1952	Dodge (Chrysler); Fisher (GM)	Plastic Dies for Steel Stampings	2	2
365	1952	Ford	Nodular Iron for Cast Crankshafts	5	2
366	1953	Buick; Cadillac; Oldsmobile (GM); Chrysler	12-Volt Electrical System	4	1
367	1953	Ford	Center-Fill Gasoline Tank	1	3
368	1953	Ford	Gate-Line Framing at Wayne Body Assembly Plant	4	2
369	1953	Ford	Suspended Clutch and Brake Pedals	1	4
370	1953	Lincoln (Ford)	Ball-Joint Front Wheel Suspension	4	3
371	1953	Lincoln (Ford)	Vented Breaker Ignition Points	2	1
372	1953	Nash-Kelvinator	Concealed Gas Filler behind Taillight	1	4
373	1953	Oldsmobile (GM)	Automatic Headlamp Dimmer	1	4
374	1953	Packard	Four-Way Power Seat Adjustment	1	4
375	1954	Chevrolet (GM); Kaiser-Fraser	Molded Plastic Body	4	2
376	1954	Chrysler	Automatic Spray Paint Guns	3	2
377	1954	Nash-Kelvinator	Air Conditioner Mounted under Hood	1	4
378	1955	Buick (GM)	Variable Pitch Blades on Torque Converter Stator (on Dynaflow automatic transmission)	1	1
379	1955	Cadillac (GM)	Curved Side Windows	1	4
380	1955	Cadillac (GM)	Dual Headlamps	1	4
381	1955	Chevrolet (GM)	Bucket Seats	1	4
382	1955	Chrysler	Automatic Transmission Selector Lever on the Dash (replaced lever control on steering column)	1	4
383	1955	Chrysler	Complete Body Assembly before Priming	3	2
384	1955	GM (Cross Company [supplier])	Segmented Transfer Lines	3	2
385	1955	GM	Wrap-Around Front Window	1	4
386	1955	Goodyear (supplier) on Packard	Tubeless Tires	1	3

Automotive Innovations 1893–1981

#	Year	Producer(s)	Innovation	Rank	Category
387	1955	Lincoln; Mercury (Ford)	Push-Button Dashboard Lubrication Control for Chassis and Suspension	1	4
388	1955	Oldsmobile (GM)	Fuel Filter inside Gasoline Tank	1	1
389	1956	Buick (GM)	Circumferential Groove on Brake Drum Interior	1	3
390	1956	Buick (GM)	Stator Member Added Between Turbine Elements (on Dynaflow automatic transmission)	1	1
391	1956	Cadillac (GM)	Quad Sealed Beam Headlights	1	4
392	1956	Cadillac (GM)	Trunk Lid Lock Control Operated from the Driver's Seat	1	4
393	1956	Chrysler	Floating Shoe, Center-Plane Brakes	1	3
394	1956	Chrysler	Transistor Car Radio	1	4
395	1956	Chrysler; Packard	Push-Button Transmission Selector	1	1
396	1956	Ford	"Deep Dish" Collapsible Steering Wheel	2	4
397	1956	Ford	Padded Sun Visors	1	4
398	1956	Ford	Safety Door Latches	1	4
399	1956	Ford	Safety Rear-View Mirror	1	4
400	1956	Packard	Electrically Controlled Door Latches	1	4
401	1956	Packard (Dana [supplier])	Non-Slip Differential	3	1
402	1956	Packard	Torsion Bar Suspension	4	3
403	1956	Studebaker	Ribbed Brake Drum	1	3
404	1957	AMC	Full Body Dip Method of Prime Painting	3	2
405	1957	AMC; Chevrolet; Pontiac (GM)	Fuel Injection	3	1
406	1957	Cadillac (GM)	Rubber-Tipped Bumper Guards	1	3
407	1957	Chevrolet (GM)	"Turbo-Guide" Automatic Transmission	2	1
408	1957	Chrysler	Rear Facing Seat in Nine-Passenger Station Wagon	1	4
409	1957	GM	Conversion of Sheet Metal Painting from Dip Process to Flow-Coat Spraying	3	2
410	1957	Mercury (Ford)	Retractable Rear Window Controlled from the Dash	1	4
411	1957	Studebaker	Limited-Slip Differential	3	1

170

Innovation in the U.S. Automobile Industry from 1893 to 1981

Automotive Innovations 1893–1981

#	Year	Producer(s)	Innovation	Rank	Category
412	1958	AMC; Mercury (Ford)	Variable-Speed Engine Fan	1	1
413	1958	Buick (GM)	Aluminum Front Brake Drums with Bonded-In Iron Liners	2	3
414	1958	Cadillac; Chevrolet; Oldsmobile; Pontiac (GM)	Three-Joint Prop Shaft	1	1
415	1958	Cadillac (GM); Chrysler	Preselect Speed Control	1	1
416	1958	Cadillac (GM); Lincoln (Ford)	Exterior Side Mirror with Adjustment Controls inside the Car	1	4
417	1958	Chrysler	Double Compound Windshield	1	4
418	1958	Ford	Floating Drum-Type Speedometer	1	4
419	1958	Ford	Push-Button, Automatic Transmission (in center of steering wheel)	1	1
420	1958	Ford	Retractable Hardtop Convertible	2	3
421	1958	Ford	Unit Air Conditioning and Heater Control	1	4
422	1958	GM	Acrylic Lacquer Optional	2	2
423	1958	GM; Ford	Air Suspension Optional	5	3
424	1958	Studebaker-Packard	Off-Center Rear Spring Mounting	1	3
425	1959	AMC	Individually Adjustable Seats	1	4
426	1959	Buick (GM)	Seat Locks	1	4
427	1959	Cadillac; Chevrolet (GM)	Plastic Bag (sleeve) Shock	1	3
428	1959	Chrysler	"Mirror-Matic" Electronic Rear-View Mirror	1	4
429	1959	Chrysler	Swivel Front Seats	1	4
430	1959	Ford	Parallel Windshield Wipers	1	4
431	1959	Ford	Thin Wall, Gray Cast Iron Engine	3	2
432	1959	Ford	Trunk Lid Catch Electrically Released inside the Car	1	4
433	1959	Ford	Vacuum Booster Fuel Pump	1	1
434	1959	GM	Metallic Brake Lining	2	3
435	1959	Oldsmobile (GM)	Flanged Brake Drum (for faster cooling)	2	3
436	1959	Pontiac (GM)	Wide-Trak Chassis	1	3

Automotive Innovations 1893–1981

#	Year	Producer(s)	Innovation	Rank	Category
437	1960	AMC	Side-Hinged Rear Station Wagon Door	1	4
438	1960	Cadillac (GM)	Automatic Vacuum Parking Brake Release	1	3
439	1960	Chevrolet (GM)	Aluminum Air-Cooled Rear-Mounted Engine	5	1
440	1960	Chevrolet (GM)	Folding Rear Seat (for luggage storage)	1	4
441	1960	Chevrolet (GM)	Swing Axle Rear Suspension	1	3
442	1960	Chevrolet (GM); Ford	Zinc Rich Paint Primer	2	2
443	1960	Chrysler	Electro-Luminescent Dashboard Lighting	1	4
444	1960	Chrysler	Four-Light Emergency Flashing System	1	4
445	1960	Chrysler	Non-Round Steering Wheel	1	4
446	1960	Chrysler	Tower Back Driver Seats	1	4
447	1960	Chrysler	Vacuum Safety Door Locks	1	4
448	1960	Ford	Anti-Theft Ignition Switch	1	4
449	1960	Ford	Automatic Convertible Top Storage	1	3
450	1960	Ford	Sliding Metal Roof Panel	1	3
451	1960	Oldsmobile (GM)	Vacuum-Operated Remote Trunk Control inside the Car	1	4
452	1960	Plymouth (Chrysler)	Alternator (AC Generator)	4	1
453	1960	Pontiac (GM)	Dual-Chambered Water Pump	1	1
454	1961	A.C. (GM)	Positive Crankcase Ventilation System	2	1
455	1961	All Producers	Resistor Cables	1	1
456	1961	AMC (Walker Mfg. and Bettinger Company [suppliers])	Ceramic-Coated Muffler and Tail Pipe	2	2
457	1961	AMC	One-Piece Fiberglass Headliner	2	2
458	1961	AMC; Chrysler	6-Cylinder Aluminum Engine	4	1
459	1961	Buick; Oldsmobile; Pontiac (GM)	Aluminum V-8 Engine	4	1
460	1961	Cadillac (GM)	Lifetime Chassis Lubrication	2	3
461	1961	Cadillac (GM)	Two-Level Air Conditioning	1	4
462	1961	Chrysler	Distributor with Nylon Breaker Points	1	1

Automotive Innovations 1893–1981

#	Year	Producer(s)	Innovation	Rank	Category
463	1961	Chrysler	Rubber-Tipped Carburetor Needle Valve	1	1
464	1961	Chrysler	Self-Tightening Power Steering Pump	1	3
465	1961	Ford	Sealed Molybdenum Lubricant	1	4
466	1961	Ford	Swing-Away Steering Wheel	1	3
467	1961	GM	First Automotive Use of Robots (used to unload a die casting machine)	3	2
468	1961	Mercury (Ford)	Cushion-Link Suspension	1	3
469	1961	Oldsmobile; Pontiac (GM)	Perimeter Frame	4	3
470	1961	Pontiac (GM)	Anodized Aluminum Bumper	1	3
471	1961	Pontiac (GM)	Cast Aluminum Wheels Optional	1	2
472	1961	Pontiac (GM)	Transaxle in Rear of Car	4	1
473	1962	All Producers	Seat Belt Anchors	1	4
474	1962	AMC	E-Stick Automatic Clutch Transmission	3	1
475	1962	AMC	Factory Front and Rear Seat Belts	1	4
476	1962	AMC	Zinc Coating by Impaction Method	2	2
477	1962	AMC; Cadillac (GM)	Dual Brakes	2	3
478	1962	Cadillac (GM)	Four-Way Taillights	1	4
479	1962	Cadillac (GM)	Front Cornering Lights	1	4
480	1962	Cadillac (GM)	Shatter-Proof Rear-View Mirror	1	4
481	1962	Chevrolet (GM)	Single-Leaf Rear Spring Suspension	1	3
482	1962	Chrysler	Rubber Isolated Steering Column	1	3
483	1962	Ford	Clutch Interlock on Manual Transmission	1	1
484	1962	Ford	30,000-Mile Engine Coolant	1	4
485	1962	Goodyear (supplier)	Polyester Fiber Cord Tire	1	3
486	1963	All Producers	Amber-Colored Turn Signals	1	4
487	1963	AMC	Transistorized Voltage Regulator	2	1
488	1963	Cadillac (GM)	Double Constant Velocity Joint at the Center	2	1
489	1963	Chrysler; Ford	Acrylic Enamel	2	2

Automotive Innovations 1893–1981

#	Year	Producer(s)	Innovation	Rank	Category
490	1963	Ford	Paint Primer Applied by Electrocoating	6	2
491	1963	GM	Automatic Transmission Console Stick Shift	1	1
492	1963	Goodyear (supplier)	Premium Inner Spare Safety Tire	1	3
493	1963	Mercury (Ford)	Simulated Wood Paneling on Station Wagons	1	3
494	1963	Ford; Pontiac (GM)	Transistorized Electronic Ignition	3	1
495	1963	Studebaker	Front-Wheel Disc Brakes	2	3
496	1964	Cadillac (GM)	Automatic Headlamp Device	1	4
497	1964	Chevrolet (GM)	Push Button Headlights	1	4
498	1964	Ford	Automatic Welding of Mustang Underbody	2	2
499	1964	Pontiac (GM)	Suspended Accelerator Pedal	1	1
500	1965	Ford	Integral Power Boost Steering Gear	1	3
501	1965	GM	Low Profile Tires	1	3
502	1965	Lincoln-Mercury (Ford)	Heating Element in Seats	1	4
503	1965	Pontiac (GM)	Rear Fender Skirts	1	3
504	1965	Pontiac (GM)	Stainless Steel on Lower Body Panels	1	3
505	1966	Ford	Dual Tailgate	1	3
506	1966	Oldsmobile (GM)	Front-Wheel Drive Reintroduced with Torsion Bar Suspension	5	3
507	1966	Pontiac (GM)	Simplified Overhead Cam Engine	3	1
508	1967	AMC; Chrysler; GM	Collapsible Steering Column	2	4
509	1967	Chrysler; Ford; GM	Weld Stud Exterior Trim Molding	2	2
510	1967	Ford	Energy-Absorbing Armrests	1	4
511	1967	Ford	Energy-Absorbing Steering Wheel Featuring a Padded Hub	2	4
512	1967	Ford	First Integrally Cast Aluminum Wheels	2	2
513	1967	Ford	Power-Operated Headrests	1	4
514	1967	GM	First Major Application of Robots in an Assembly Plant (used for spot welding)	5	2
515	1967	Oldsmobile (GM)	Engine Pre-Heater Optional	1	1

Automotive Innovations 1893–1981

#	Year	Producer(s)	Innovation	Rank	Category
516	1967	Oldsmobile (GM)	Ultra-High Voltage Ignition Capacitor System	1	1
517	1967	Pontiac (GM)	Recessed Windshield Wipers	1	4
518	1968	All Producers	Safety Front Shoulder Harness	1	4
519	1968	AMC	Headlamp Warning Buzzer	1	4
520	1968	Chrysler	Washer-Wiper for Tailgate Window on Station Wagons	1	4
521	1968	Ford	"Controlled Crush" Front End	4	3
522	1968	Ford	Reflective Painted Wheels	1	4
523	1968	Ford	Reflective Racing Strips along the Rocker Panels	1	4
524	1968	Ford	Squeeze-Type Door Handles	1	4
525	1968	Ford; GM	Child Restraint Seat	1	4
526	1968	Goodyear (supplier) on Lincoln (Ford)	Double-Chambered Captive-Air Tire for Safety	1	3
527	1968	Lincoln (Ford)	Transistorized Headlamp Dimmer	1	4
528	1968	Oldsmobile (GM)	Horn Ring inside Steering Wheel	1	4
529	1968	Pontiac (GM)	Deflated Spare Tire with a Charge of Freon Gas for Inflation	1	3
530	1968	Pontiac (GM)	Energy-Absorbing Bumper	3	3
531	1968	Pontiac (GM)	Integrated Micro-Circuit Used in Electrical Charging System	1	1
532	1969	AMC; Lincoln (Ford)	Fiberglass Bias-Belted Tires	1	3
533	1969	AMC	Translucent Battery Case	1	4
534	1969	Chevrolet (GM)	Headlamp Washer	1	4
535	1969	Chevrolet (GM)	Liquid Tire Chain	1	4
536	1969	Chevrolet	Station Wagon Rear Air Spoiler	1	4
537	1969	Dodge (Chrysler)	Auxiliary Headlight	1	4
538	1969	Ford	Energy-Absorbing Frame	3	3
539	1969	Ford	Skid Control Braking System	2	3
540	1969	GM	Locking Steering Column	1	4
541	1969	GM (Digital [supplier])	Programmable Control	5	2
542	1969	GM	Safety Door Beams	2	2
543	1969	GM	Energy-Absorbing Steering Column—Second Generation	2	4

Automotive Innovations 1893–1981

#	Year	Producer(s)	Innovation	Rank	Category
544	1969	Pontiac (GM)	Radio Antenna Imbedded in Windshield	1	4
545	1970	All California Models	Evaporative Fuel Controls (for gas tank and carburetor)	2	4
546	1970	AMC	Granulating Safety Windshield	2	4
547	1970	AMC; Ford; Chrysler	High-Back Bucket Seats with Integral Head Restraints	1	4
548	1970	Cadillac (GM)	Electrically Operated Sunroof	1	4
549	1970	Cadillac (GM)	Signal-Seeking Stereo Radio	1	4
550	1970	Cadillac (GM); Ford	Tamper-Proof Odometer	1	4
551	1970	Chrysler	Roll-Over Safety Structure under the Roof Panel	2	4
552	1970	Ford	Adjustable Station Wagon Roof Rack	1	4
553	1970	Ford	Front-End Accessory Drive	1	4
554	1970	GM	Automated and Computerized Assembly of Vega at Lordstown, PA.	6	2
555	1970	GM	Automatic Seat-Back Release	1	4
556	1970	GM	Transmission-Controlled Spark System	1	1
557	1970	GM	Turn-Signal Operated Washer-Wipe	1	4
558	1970	Mercury (Ford)	Freon-Filled Shock Absorber	1	3
559	1970	Oldsmobile (GM)	Inside Hood Latch Release	1	4
560	1970	Pontiac (GM)	Plastic Gas Tank on Station Wagons	1	4
561	1970	Pontiac (GM)	Rear Deck Air Foil	1	4
562	1970	Chevrolet; Pontiac (GM)	"Double Shell Top" Roof	2	3
563	1970	Chevrolet; Pontiac (GM)	First Full Foam Seats	1	4
564	1971	AMC	Counterbalanced Rear Window Lift Gate	1	4
565	1971	AMC	Ventilating Rotor Front Power Disc Brakes	1	3
566	1971	Buick (GM)	Computerized Anti-Wheel Spin System	2	3
567	1971	Buick (GM)	Single-Piece Cast Steering Knuckle	1	2
568	1971	Chevrolet (GM)	Bolt-On Fenders and Front Body Panels	1	2

176

Automotive Innovations 1893–1981

#	Year	Producer(s)	Innovation	Rank	Category
569	1971	Chevrolet (GM)	Electric Fuel Pump in Gasoline Tank	1	1
570	1971	Chevrolet (GM)	Refined Front Suspension	2	3
571	1971	Chevrolet (GM)	Sleeveless, 4-Cylinder Aluminum Engine (with cast iron head)	2	1
572	1971	Chrysler	Four-Wheel, Anti-Skid Braking System	2	3
573	1971	Chrysler	Optional Block Heater	1	1
574	1971	Chrysler	Washer System for Concealed Headlamps	1	4
575	1971	Delco (GM)	Side-Terminal Battery	1	1
576	1971	Ford	Automatic Temperature Control Air Conditioning	1	4
577	1971	Ford	Station Wagon Tailgate Wiper-Washer	1	4
578	1971	GM	Disappearing Tailgate Window	1	4
579	1971	Pontiac (GM)	Maintenance-Free Sealed Battery	2	1
580	1971	Pontiac (GM)	Sheet-Molding Compound (SMC) Plastic Front End Panel	3	2
581	1972	All Producers	Buzzer and Light Seat Belt Reminder	1	4
582	1972	Chrysler; Pontiac (GM)	Solid-State Ignition System (eliminated points and condenser)	4	1
583	1972	Lincoln (Ford)	3-Quart Plastic Radiator Overflow Reservoir	1	4
584	1972	Ford	Seat Belt Engine-Interlock System	1	4
585	1973	All Producers	5 and 2½ Mph Impact Bumpers	2	3
586	1973	AMC	Single Unit Rear Window and Trunk	2	4
587	1973	Chevrolet (GM)	Swing-Out Bucket Seats	1	4
588	1973	Chrysler	Electronic Digital Clock	1	1
589	1973	Ford	Aluminum Bumper Reinforcements	2	3
590	1973	Ford	Forged Aluminum Wheels	1	2
591	1973	GM	Colonnade Hardtop	1	3
592	1973	GM	On-Board Diagnostic System	3	4
593	1973	Lincoln (Ford)	Power Mini-Vent Side Windows	1	4
594	1974	AMC	Free-Standing Front and Rear Bumpers	1	3

177

Automotive Innovations 1893–1981

#	Year	Producer(s)	Innovation	Rank	Category
595	1974	Chevrolet (GM)	Front Disc Brake Wear Sensors	1	3
596	1974	Chrysler	Four-Wheel Power Disc Brakes	2	3
597	1974	Chrysler	Windshield Wiper Fluid Gauge	1	4
598	1974	Dodge (Chrysler)	Fuel and Electrical Alert System	1	4
599	1975	Chevrolet (GM) (Reynolds [supplier])	Aluminum Bumper	2	3
600	1975	Chrysler	Aluminum Brake Shields	1	2
601	1975	Ford	Aluminum Intake Manifold	2	2
602	1975	GM	Oxidation Catalyst (oxidized HC and CO)	5	1
603	1975	Oldsmobile (GM)	Aluminum Inner Hood Panel	2	2
604	1976	Chrysler	Electronic Engine Controls (analog, lean-burn, spark advance system)	5	1
605	1977	Buick; Chevrolet (GM)	High Strength, Low Alloy (HSLA) Steel Face Bar for Bumpers	1	2
606	1977	Chrysler	Ultra-High Strength (UHS) Steel Door Impact Beams	2	2
607	1977	Delco (GM)	Computer Vision Inspection Station	2	2
608	1977	Ford; GM	Partial Plastic Liners on Front Fenders	1	3
609	1977	GM	Aluminum Loading Door on Station Wagons	2	2
610	1977	GM	"MISAR" Spark Advance System	5	1
611	1977	Pontiac (GM)	Reaction-Injected-Molded Plastic Bumper Fascia	1	2
612	1978	Cadillac (GM); Lincoln (Ford); Oldsmobile (GM)	All-Aluminum Passenger Car Hood	3	2
613	1978	Ford	Aluminum Power-Steering Pump Housing	2	2
614	1978	Ford	Aluminum Rack-and-Pinion Steering Gear Housing	2	2
615	1978	Ford	Electronic Engine Control Series	3	1
616	1978	Ford; GM	Three-Way Catalytic Converter	3	1
617	1979	Dodge (Chrysler)	Aluminum Cylinder Heads	3	1

178

Automotive Innovations 1893–1981

#	Year	Producer(s)	Innovation	Rank	Category
618	1979	Ford	Aluminum Brake Master Cylinder	2	3
619	1980	Ford	Automatic Overdrive Transmission	4	1
620	1980	Ford	Magnesium Vacuum Advance Housing on V-8 Engines	2	2
621	1980	Ford	Magnesium Window Sail Mirror Plate	1	2
622	1980	Ford	Mini-Fuse Panel and Plug-In Fuse	2	4
623	1980	Lincoln	Magnesium Steering Column Lock Housing	1	2
624	1981	AMC	"Select Drive"	2	1
625	1981	Cadillac (GM)	Valve Selector Device on V-8 Engine	3	1
626	1981	Ford	Magnesium Louver for Rear-Quarter Window	1	2
627	1981	Ford	Magnesium Rear-Quarter Window Molding	1	2
628	1981	Ford	Painted Magnesium Exterior Mirror Arm	1	2
629	1981	GM	Laser Robotic Scanners in Assembly Plants	3	2
630	1981	GM	Programmable Robot Painter	4	2
631	1981	GM	"Computer Command Control"	4	1

TABLE D.2

Index of Transilience for Automotive Innovations

Epoch (Year)	Total Obs[1]	Drive Train Index[2]	Drive Train Smooth[3]	Drive Train #	Process Index	Process Smooth	Process #	Chassis Index	Chassis Smooth	Chassis #	Other Index	Other Smooth	Other #
1894	9	101.00	101.00	7	36.00	36.00	1	4.00	4.00	1	0.00	0.00	0
1899	18	49.00	101.00	7	20.00	36.00	2	75.00	63.00	7	5.00	5.00	2
1902	34	211.00	91.00	20	75.00	36.00	3	63.00	63.00	7	7.00	5.00	4
1905	19	81.00	91.00	12	4.00	65.00	1	12.00	12.00	6	0.00	2.00	0
1908	20	91.00	81.00	9	83.00	65.00	6	3.00	12.00	3	2.00	2.00	2
1911	17	54.00	81.00	5	65.00	65.00	2	58.00	35.00	6	4.00	4.00	4
1914	27	107.00	54.00	7	107.00	45.00	6	35.00	35.00	6	11.00	4.00	8
1917	12	49.00	49.00	5	45.00	45.00	2	6.00	13.00	3	2.00	7.00	2
1920	14	36.00	49.00	3	39.00	46.00	5	13.00	13.00	2	7.00	7.00	4
1923	24	116.00	78.00	8	111.00	46.00	7	98.00	35.00	5	19.00	7.00	4
1926	20	78.00	78.00	6	46.00	46.00	4	35.00	35.00	6	4.00	4.00	4
1929	14	47.00	47.00	5	42.00	69.00	4	23.00	23.00	5	0.00	4.00	0
1932	28	103.00	40.00	16	69.00	69.00	7	9.00	23.00	3	5.00	5.00	2
1935	30	37.00	40.00	5	137.00	69.00	8	113.00	29.00	13	7.00	7.00	4
1938	24	40.00	40.00	5	13.00	25.00	2	29.00	29.00	9	14.00	7.00	8
1943	16	54.00	40.00	3	25.00	25.00	1	65.00	29.00	6	6.00	6.00	6
1944	1	0.00	1.00	0	4.00	25.00	1	0.00	0.00	0	0.00	3.00	0
1947	11	1.00	1.00	1	27.00	27.00	3	34.00	26.00	4	3.00	3.00	3
1950	24	72.00	20.00	6	91.00	70.00	5	22.00	26.00	4	12.00	5.00	9
1953	15	20.00	35.00	2	70.00	70.00	5	26.00	26.00	3	5.00	12.00	5
1956	34	35.00	35.00	8	36.00	36.00	4	21.00	26.00	6	19.00	19.00	16
1959	42	47.00	47.00	8	17.00	36.00	3	48.00	37.00	12	19.00	19.00	19
1962	42	83.00	47.00	13	62.00	36.00	7	37.00	37.00	13	9.00	9.00	9
1965	12	10.00	10.00	2	4.00	47.00	1	30.00	37.00	6	3.00	9.00	3
1968	37	3.00	10.00	3	62.00	47.00	5	41.00	30.00	7	31.00	31.00	22
1971	40	28.00	26.00	7	47.00	47.00	4	18.00	19.00	6	32.00	31.00	23
1974	19	26.00	28.00	2	10.00	31.00	4	19.00	18.00	7	17.00	17.00	6
1977	13	68.00	54.00	4	31.00	31.00	8	1.00	4.00	1	0.00	4.00	0
1980	15	54.00	54.00	5	34.00	34.00	8	4.00	4.00	1	4.00	4.00	1

SOURCE: See text of appendix C.

NOTES: 1. "Total Obs" stands for Number of innovations observed; "#" stands for the number of innovations in a category.
2. "Index" is the sum of squared weights attached to each innovation.
3. "Smooth" is the smoothed version of "Index" using median-removal technique.

Notes

Chapter 1

1. These distinctions were first developed in William J. Abernathy, Kim B. Clark, and Alan M. Kantrow, "The New Industrial Competition," *Harvard Business Review* (September–October, 1981), pp. 68–81.

2. F. Scott Fitzgerald, *Tender Is the Night* (1934; reprint ed., New York: Charles Scribner's Sons, 1962), pp. 54–55.

3. This is the theme of Robert H. Hayes and William J. Abernathy, "Managing Our Way to Economic Decline," *Harvard Business Review* (July–August, 1980), pp. 67–77.

4. F. Scott Fitzgerald, *The Great Gatsby* (1925; reprint ed., New York: Charles Scribner's Sons, 1953), p. 59.

5. Alfred P. Sloan, *My Years with General Motors* (1963; reprint ed.; New York: Doubleday & Company, Inc., 1972), pp. 185–187.

6. These observations are based on numerous discussions with executives from a variety of American industries. Corroborating evidence has also been developed in a survey of senior corporate executives conducted in the spring and summer of 1982. For more detail on this survey see Russell Radford et al., "The View From the Top: Executive Perspectives on the New Industrial Competition" (Harvard Business School Working Paper, 1983).

7. Cited in James Fallows, "American Industry: What Ails It, How to Save It," *Atlantic Monthly* (September, 1980), p. 36.

8. Fallows, "American Industry," p. 47.

9. Robert H. Hayes and Kim B. Clark, "Sanyo Manufacturing Corp." (Harvard Business School Case no. 0–682–045, 1982).

Chapter 2

1. See Louis T. Wells, Jr., "The International Product Life Cycle and United States Regulation of the Automobile Industry," in Douglas H. Ginsburg and William J. Abernathy, eds., *Government, Technology, and the Future of the Automobile* (New York: McGraw-Hill, 1980), pp. 270–304.

2. Edward M. Graham, "Technological Innovation and the Dynamics of the U.S. Competitive Advantage in International Trade," in Christopher T. Hill and James M. Utterback, eds., *Tech-*

nological Innovation for a Dynamic Economy (Elmsford, New York: Pergamon Press, 1979), p. 152.

3. For a more in-depth discussion of this idea, see Robert B. Reich, "Why the U.S. Needs an Industrial Policy," *Harvard Business Review* (January–February, 1982), pp. 74–81, and Robert A. Leone and Stephen P. Bradley, "Toward an Effective Industrial Policy," *Harvard Business Review* (November–December, 1981), pp. 91–97.

4. A clear statement of this view is contained in Abraham Katz, Statement of Abraham Katz, Assistant Secretary of Commerce for International Economic Policy, before the Subcommittee on Trade of the House Ways and Means Committee (March, 1980).

5. See Louis T. Wells, Jr., *Product Life Cycle and International Trade* (Boston: Harvard Graduate School of Business Administration, Division of Research, 1972), and Raymond Vernon, *Storm Over the Multinationals: The Real Issues* (Cambridge: Harvard University Press, 1977).

6. William J. Abernathy and Phillip L. Townsend, "Technology, Productivity and Process Change," *Technological Forecasting and Social Change* VII, 4 (1975), pp. 379–396. For additional development of these ideas see William J. Abernathy and James M. Utterback, "Patterns of Industrial Innovation," *Technology Review* (June–July, 1978), pp. 40–47.

7. Ideas along these lines have been developed by Robert H. Hayes and Steven C. Wheelright in two articles: "The Dynamics of Process-Product Life Cycles," *Harvard Business Review* (March–April, 1979), pp. 127–136, and "Link Manufacturing Process and Product Life Cycles," *Harvard Business Review* (January–February, 1979), pp. 133–140.

8. This is the central theme of William J. Abernathy, *The Productivity Dilemma* (Baltimore: Johns Hopkins University Press, 1978).

9. For more detail on the experience curve, see The Boston Consulting Group, *Perspectives on Experience* (1968; reprint ed., Boston: The Boston Consulting Group, 1972).

10. Walter Kiechell III, "The Decline of the Experience Curve," *Fortune* (October 5, 1981), p. 140.

11. An early statement of these problems can be found in William J. Abernathy and Kenneth Wayne, "Limits of the Learning Curve," *Harvard Business Review* (September–October, 1974), pp. 109–119.

12. See, for example, Abernathy and Townsend, "Technology Productivity and Process Change."

13. The notion of "design concept" can be found in Abernathy, *Productivity Dilemma,* chapters 2 and 7, and in Kim B. Clark, "Competition, Technical Diversity and Radical Innovation in the U.S. Auto Industry," in Richard S. Rosenbloom, *Research on Technological Innovation Management and Policy* (Greenwich, Connecticut: JAI Press, 1983).

14. For ideas related to the notion of a "design hierarchy," see David L. Marples, "The Decisions of Engineering Design," *IRE Transactions of Engineering Management* 2 (June, 1961), pp. 55–71, and Christopher Alexander, *Notes on the Synthesis of Form* (Cambridge: Harvard University Press, 1964).

15. The connection between product and process innovation is developed in detail in Abernathy and Utterback, "Patterns of Industrial Innovation," pp. 40–47.

16. The importance of uncertainty in driving competition is developed in Clark, "Competition, Technical Diversity and Radical Innovation." It is also an important aspect of the models developed by Nelson and Winter. See, for example, Richard R. Nelson and Sidney G. Winter, "In Search of Useful Theory of Innovation," *Research Policy* VI (1977), pp. 36–75.

Chapter 3

1. For a more in-depth discussion of the concepts developed in this chapter, see William J. Abernathy and John E. Corcoran, "Relearning From The Olds Masters: Contemporary Implica-

tions of the American System of Manufacturing" (Harvard Business School Working Paper, 1982).

2. Report from the Select Committee on Scientific Instruction, Parliamentary Papers, 15 (1867–1868) Q 6722, cited in Nathan Rosenberg, ed., *The American System of Manufacturers: The Report of the Committee on the Machinery of the United States 1855 and the Special Reports of George Wallis and Joseph Whitworth 1854* (Edinburgh: Edinburgh University Press, 1969), p. 15.

3. See, for example, John E. Sawyer, "The Social Basis of the American System of Manufacturing," *Journal of Economic History* XIV, 4 (1954), pp. 361–379.

4. Alfred D. Chandler, Jr., *The Visible Hand: The Managerial Revolution in American Business* (Cambridge: Harvard University Press, 1977), p. 271.

5. John Scott, *Genius Rewarded: The Story of the Sewing Machine* (New York: John J. Caulon, 1880), p. 48.

6. Nathan Rosenberg, ed., *The American System*, p. 125.

7. Nathan Rosenberg, *Perspectives on Technology* (Cambridge: Cambridge University Press, 1976), p. 162.

8. Alfred D. Chandler, Jr., ed., *Giant Enterprise: Ford, General Motors, and the Automobile Industry* (New York: Harcourt, Brace & World, Inc., 1964), p. 212.

9. Allan Nevins, *Ford: The Times, the Man, the Company* (New York: Charles Scribner's Sons, 1954), p. 212.

Chapter 4

1. For a review of national policies that affected international trade in automobiles from the 1890s to the present, see Mira Wilkins, "Multinational Automobile Enterprises and Regulation: An Historical Overview," in Douglas H. Ginsburg and William J. Abernathy, eds., *Government, Technology and the Future of the Automobile* (New York: McGraw–Hill, 1980), pp. 221–258.

2. Automobile Panel, Committee on Technology and International Economic and Trade Issues, National Academy of Engineering (prepared by Kim B. Clark), *The Competitive Status of the Influence of Technology in Determining International Competitive Advantage* (Washington, D.C.: National Academy of Science, 1982), pp. 53–55.

3. The number of equivalent firms is calculated as the inverse of the Herfindahl index, a description of which may be found in Frederic M. Scherer, *Industrial Market Structure and Economic Performance* (Chicago: Rand-McNally Publishing Co., 1980), p. 51.

4. Ford's integration of its European operations is discussed in Yves L. Doz, "Competition in Worldwide Industries. The Automobile Industry" (unpublished paper, 1979).

5. Mergers, alliances, and coalitions are discussed in National Academy of Engineering, *Competitive Status*, pp. 62–64, and in Mark Fuller, "Note on the World Auto Industry in Transition" (Harvard Business School Case no. NCA–382–122, 1982).

6. The story of the small car in the U.S. market is discussed in Lawrence J. White, *The Automobile Industry Since 1945* (Cambridge: Harvard University Press, 1971), pp. 177–188.

7. For a discussion of the Brush Runabout and other early cars, see James J. Flink, *America Adopts the Automobile, 1895–1910* (Cambridge: MIT Press, 1970).

8. Allan Nevins and Frank E. Hill, *Ford: Decline and Rebirth, 1933–1962* (New York: Charles Scribner's Sons, 1963), pp. 117–119, as cited in William J. Abernathy, *The Productivity Dilemma* (Baltimore: Johns Hopkins University Press, 1978), p. 28.

9. See "Annual Automotive Issue," *Consumer Reports* (April, 1960).

10. Karen Tracy, "Note on Automobile Safety Regulation" (unpublished report, Harvard Business School, 1978).

Chapter 5

1. For a brief discussion of the early failure of Toyota automobiles in the U.S. market, see Shotaro Kamiya, *My Life with Toyota* (Tokyo: Toyota Motor Sales Co., 1976), pp. 77–80.

2. Abraham Katz, Statement of Abraham Katz, Assistant Secretary of Commerce for International Economic Policy, before the Subcommittee on Trade of the House Ways and Means Committee (March, 1980).

3. Ford Motor Company, *State of the U.S. Automobile Industry* (Dearborn: Ford Motor Company, 1978).

4. Eric J. Toder, *Trade Policy and the U.S. Automobile Industry* (New York: Praeger Publishers, 1978), pp. 150–155.

5. William J. Abernathy, *The Productivity Dilemma* (Baltimore: Johns Hopkins University Press, 1978), pp. 178–180.

6. Data on automobile industry productivity are published by the Bureau of Labor Statistics, U.S. Department of Labor. See, for example, Bureau of Labor Statistics, U.S. Department of Labor, *Handbook of Labor Statistics* (Washington, D.C.: U.S. Government Printing Office, 1974), p. 187.

7. Great Britain House of Commons, *Fourteenth Report From The Expenditure Committee—The Motor Vehicle Industry,* Minutes Taken Before The Trade and Industry Sub-Committee (London: Her Majesty's Stationery Office, 1975), p. 83.

8. See Appendix B for sources on U.S. and Japanese wage rates.

9. S. L. (Red) Binstock, "Americans Express Dissatisfaction with Quality of U.S. Goods," *Quality Progress* (January, 1981), pp. 12–14.

10. Warranty cost data are provided in William J. Abernathy et al., *Productivity and Comparative Cost Advantages: Some Estimates for Major Automotive Producers* (unpublished report; Cambridge: Department of Transportation, 1980), p. 60.

Chapter 6

1. See, for example, Horace L. Arnold and Fay L. Faurote, *Ford Methods and the Ford Shops* (New York: The Engineering Magazine Company, 1915).

2. William J. Abernathy, *The Productivity Dilemma* (Baltimore: Johns Hopkins University Press, 1978), pp. 22–24.

3. Arnold and Faurote describe the process at Ford with its extensive specialization. See Arnold and Faurote, *Ford Methods,* pp. 130–158, as cited in Abernathy, *The Productivity Dilemma,* p. 24. See also Stephen Meyer, *The Five Dollar Day* (Albany: State University of New York Press, 1981), pp. 9–37.

4. Meyer, *The Five Dollar Day,* pp. 56–57 discusses the importance of the production clerk at Ford.

5. Henry Ford, in collaboration with Samuel Crowther, *My Life and Work* (Garden City, New York: Doubleday, Page & Company, 1922), pp. 59–60, as cited in Alfred D. Chandler, Jr., *Giant Enterprise* (New York: Harcourt, Brace & World, 1964), p. 39.

6. The evolution of the foreman's job is discussed in W. Earl Sasser, Jr. and Frank S. Leonard, "Let First-Level Supervisors Do Their Job," *Harvard Business Review* (March–April, 1980), pp. 113–121.

7. Our field research in Japan is discussed more fully in William J. Abernathy and Kim B. Clark, "Notes on a Trip to Japan: Concepts and Interpretations" (Harvard Business School Working Paper, 1982).

8. Kim B. Clark, "Toyo Kogyo Co. Ltd. (A) and (B)" (Harvard Business School Case nos. 9–682–092, 1982, and 9–682–093, 1982).

9. Just-in-time inventory systems as developed and practiced in Japan are discussed in Robert W. Hall, *Driving the Productivity Machine: Production and Control in Japan* (Falls Church, Va.: American Production and Inventory Control Society, 1981), and Yasuhiro Monden, "What Makes the Toyota Production System Really Tick?" *Industrial Engineering* (January, 1981), pp. 36–46.

10. See, for example, Richard B. Chase and Nicholas J. Aquilano, *Production and Operations Management* (Homewood, Ill.: R.D. Irwin, Inc., 1977), pp. 368–419.

11. Clark, "Toyo Kogyo Co. Ltd. (B) (Case no. 9–682–093), p. 4.

12. The literal meaning of *Jidoka* is automation with a human face. At Toyota it has come to mean "making problems visible."

13. The importance of visual communication in Japan is emphasized by Peter Drucker, *Men, Ideas and Politics* (New York: Harper & Row, 1971), chap. 20.

14. The kanban system as practiced at Toyota is discussed at length in Shigeo Shingo, *Study of Toyota Production System* (Tokyo: Japan Management Association, 1981).

15. Robert H. Hayes, "Why Japanese Factories Work," *Harvard Business Review* (July–August, 1981), pp. 57–66.

16. A typical newspaper article is "Robots Do the Work on Datsuns," *Milwaukee Journal* (April 23, 1980).

17. A comparison of Ford's approach and the approach at Toyota is presented in Shigeo Shingo, *Study of Toyota Production System*, pp. 138–145.

18. A discussion of the integration achieved at the Rouge plant is contained in Allan Nevins and Frank Hill, *Ford: Expansion and Challenge, 1915–1933* (New York: Charles Scribner's Sons, 1957), pp. 279–299. Data on cost, labor content, and throughput time can be found in Accounting Data and Cost Studies, Ford Archives, Henry Ford Museum, Greenfield Village, Dearborn, Michigan.

19. Anne Jardin, *The First Henry Ford: A Study in Personality and Business Leadership* (Cambridge: MIT Press, 1970), p. 204.

20. John R. Lee, "The So-Called Profit Sharing System in the Ford Plant, *Annals, American Academy of Political and Social Science* 64 (May, 1916), p. 299, as cited in Chandler, *Giant Enterprise*, p. 189.

21. Meyer, *Five Dollar Day*, p. 10.

22. Chandler, *Giant Enterprise*, pp. 214–218.

Chapter 7

1. We are indebted to our colleague W. Earl Sasser, Jr. for this example.

2. The Japanese manufacturers we interviewed regarded quality circles as one of the last things to be done after the foundations of the production system had been established. This view is consistent with the findings of Robert H. Hayes, "Why Japanese Factories Work," *Harvard Business Review* (July–August, 1981), pp. 57–66.

3. See Alfred D. Chandler, Jr., *Giant Enterprise: Ford, General Motors, and the Automobile Industry* (New York: Harcourt, Brace & World, Inc., 1964), pp. 194–229, for references on Harry Bennett and The Service Bureau.

185

4. Chandler, *Giant Enterprise,* p. 215.

5. Chandler, *Giant Enterprise,* p. 219. For a listing of bargaining gains, see United Auto Workers, *Collective Bargaining Gains by Date of Settlement: UAW-General Motors, 1937–1982* (Detroit: United Auto Workers Research Department, 1981).

6. George C. Lodge, "Individualism, Interest Groups, Contracts and Consensus at GM, 1908–1972" (Harvard Business School Case no. 9–373–017, 1973), p. 13, citing a statement by Alfred P. Sloan, *New York Times* (January 5, 1937).

7. Tom Mahoney, *The Story of George Romney: Builder, Salesman, Crusader* (New York: Harper & Brothers, 1960), p. 162, as cited in Robert M. MacDonald, *Collective Bargaining in the Automotive Industry* (New Haven: Yale University Press, 1963), p. 368.

8. MacDonald, *Collective Bargaining,* p. 319, as quoted from a speech before the Detroit Kiwanis Club, August 14, 1944.

9. For a summary of the actions of Ford and Chrysler in the 1950s, see MacDonald, *Collective Bargaining,* pp. 311–355, and the references cited there.

10. Bert Specter and Paul R. Lawrence, "General Motors and the United Auto Workers" (Harvard Business School Case no. 9–481–142, 1982), p. 4.

11. C. Wickham Skinner and Frank S. Leonard, "Kalamazoo Plant" (Harvard Business School Case no. 9–679–106, 1979). This case provides a graphic example of the adversarial nature of labor-management relations in the auto industry.

12. Many company unions in Japan are company sponsored, while others are independent of the company even though bargaining occurs on a company basis. For the former, the union is in fact, and not just in appearance, an arm of the personnel department. In the latter situation, the union pursues a more independent course. For a more in-depth analysis of unionism in Japan, see Robert J. Ballon, *The Japanese Employee* (Tokyo: Charles F. Tuttle Co., 1969), chaps. 9, 10, and 11.

13. There have been numerous articles on the QWL programs at General Motors. See, for example, Robert H. Guest, "Quality of Work Life—Learning from Tarrytown," *Harvard Business Review* (July–August 1979), pp. 76–87, and William F. Dowling, "At General Motors: System 4 Builds Performance and Profits," *Organizational Dynamics* (Winter, 1975), pp. 23–38.

14. Bert Spector and Michael Beer, "A Note on the 1982 Automobile Negotiations," (Harvard Business School Case no. 0–482–103, 1982), p. 4.

15. Spector and Beer, "A Note on 1982 Negotiations," p. 5.

Chapter 8

1. The processes that advertising agencies go through to develop advertising supports this view. See, for example, Maurice I. Mandell, *Advertising* (Englewood Cliffs, N.J.: Prentice-Hall, Inc., 3d ed., 1980), chaps. 7 and 8.

2. A classic discussion of manipulative advertising can be found in John Kenneth Galbraith, *The New Industrial State* (Boston: Houghton Mifflin, 1967), chap. XVIII.

3. The concept of implicit prices as we use it here has been developed in the economics literature on hedonic prices. See, for example, Sherwin Rosen, "Hedonic Prices and Implicit Markets: Product Differentiation in Price Competition," *Journal of Political Economy* (January–February, 1974), pp. 34–55.

4. There is a large literature on hedonic price analysis. See, for example, Zvi Griliches and Makoto Ohta, "Automobile Prices Revisited: Extension of the Hedonic Hypotheses," in Nester Terlecky, ed., *Household Production and Consumption* (New York: National Bureau of Economic Research, 1975). A more technical discussion of the price analysis we used may be found in Kim

B. Clark, "Competition, Technical Diversity and Radical Innovation in the U.S. Auto Industry," in Richard S. Rosenbloom, *Research on Technological Innovation Management and Policy* (Greenwich, Conn.: JAI Press, 1983).

5. Recent research by James Kahn has shown that the market valuation of used cars has responded to changes in gasoline prices. His work did not, however, focus on the kind of technology characteristics we examined here. See James Kahn, "The Adjustment of the Used Automobile Market to Gasoline Price Shocks: An Asset Model Approach," Harvard College Senior Honors Thesis (March, 1981).

Chapter 9

1. John E. Tilton, *International Diffusion of Technology: The Case of Semiconductors* (Washington, D.C.: Brookings Institution, 1971), pp. 16–95.

2. The importance of the cumulative effect of incremental innovation has been documented by Samuel Hollander, *The Sources of Increased Efficiency: A Study of DuPont Rayon Plants* (Cambridge: MIT Press, 1965).

3. William J. Abernathy and James M. Utterback, "Patterns of Industrial Innovation," *Technology Review* (June–July, 1978), p. 43.

4. Michael E. Porter, et al., "The Chain Saw Industry in 1974," and "The Chain Saw Industry in 1978" (Harvard Business School Case nos. 9–379–157, 1979, and 9–379–176, 1979) provide an account of the changes in the chain saw industry following the oil shock of 1973.

5. Robert Sobel, *IBM: Colossus in Transition* (New York: Truman Talley Books—Times Books, 1981), pp. 208–232.

6. The plastic engine is described in "What—A Plastic Engine!?" *Automotive Industries* (December, 1980), pp. 40–43.

7. Interviews with industry development personnel.

8. John McElroy, "The 80s: Seven New Engines Make the Scene," *Automotive Industries* (October, 1979), pp. 85–94.

Chapter 10

1. See Richard S. Rosenbloom, "Ampex (A)" (Harvard Business School Case no. 9–658–002, 1958), and Margaret B. W. Graham, "Ampex Corporation: Product Matrix Engineering" (Harvard Business School Case no. 9–680–142, 1980).

2. William J. Abernathy and Richard S. Rosenbloom, "The Institutional Climate for Innovation in Industry: The Role of Management" (Harvard Business School Working Paper, 1980). For additional analysis of these phenomena, see Margaret B. W. Graham's forthcoming book, tentatively titled *The RCA Video Disc: Innovation in Context.*

3. Burton H. Klein, *Dynamic Economics* (Cambridge: Harvard University Press, 1977), chapter 2 contains an analysis of innovation in jet engines.

4. Wallace K. Ferguson, "Toward the Modern State," in *The Renaissance: Six Essays* (New York: Harper & Row, 1960), pp. 3–4.

Appendix A

1. The influence of technology on market structure is discussed in David Haddock, "Determinants of Industrial Concentration in the United States Automobile Industry, 1907–1979" (unpublished paper March, 1980). See also Morton I. Kamien and Nancy L. Schwartz, *Market Structure and Innovation* (Cambridge: Cambridge University Press, 1982), pp. 49–104, where economic research on this topic is discussed.

Index

Index